# MISCONCEPTIONS

## A GUIDE TO THE WORLD'S MOST POPULAR

### *Myths*

TIM RAYBORN

WHALEN
BOOK·WORKS

Kennebunkport, Maine

*To Eric Sutton, who knows it all!*

*Misconceptions: A Guide to the World's Most Popular Myths*

13-digit ISBN: 978-1-95151-104-3
10-digit ISBN: 1-951511-04-2

This book may be ordered by mail from the publisher. Please include $5.99 for postage and handling. Please support your local bookseller first!

Books published by Whalen Book Works are available at special discounts when purchased in bulk. For more information, please email us at info@whalenbookworks.com.

Whalen Book Works
68 North Street
Kennebunkport, ME 04046
www.whalenbookworks.com

Cover and interior design by Melissa Gerber

Typography: Gotham, ITC Caslon 224, Burford, Trade Gothic, Citrus Gothic, Adobe Caslon Bodoni Poster, Golden Hills, Bodoni, Fontbox Boathouse, and Anthology.

Printed in China
1 2 3 4 5 6 7 8 9 0

First Edition

# CONTENTS

# Introduction

**We've all absorbed lots of information and trivia over the years,** and some of it gets stored away in our brains to be let out again as anecdotes at parties, when we're giving a speech, or just when we're trying to look impressive. Most people have at least a small stack of useless facts that they like to share once in a while, but there's a problem: some of the most cherished bits of information we think we know are actually not true at all. Quite a lot of them, in fact.

This little book is a compendium of misconceptions, urban legends, and things that people just plain get wrong, but usually don't bother to check up on. You probably know a lot of these, and you might be surprised at just how wrong some of our preconceived notions about the truth actually are. This collection of interesting facts will arm you with a whole new arsenal of cool things that you can bring out when the time is right, and maybe once in a while correct a mistake when you hear it.

Covering history, science, the natural world, and popular culture, here is a great collection of new facts that in many ways are even more interesting than the misconceptions you've had about them so far. Impress your friends and family, win a few bets, or just increase your knowledge of this weird and wonderful world we live in!

# CHAPTER 1:
## History

**History is full of mysteries,** and there's no way we can keep track of all of them, which is why most historians specialize in one era, area, or a similar grouping of topics to study. Unfortunately, history is also a repository for every kind of misconception you can imagine. This problem can be due to a lack of historical sources, or just popular myths and urban legends that grow up over time and take hold in the popular imagination, long after the truth has been buried in dusty old books in a library. This chapter explores some of the more glaring misconceptions about the past and tries to set the (historical) record straight.

# George Washington did not have wooden teeth.

He did wear dentures, since he had lost almost all of his teeth by the time he became president. He had sets that were made of ivory, gold, brass, animal teeth, and human teeth taken from slaves. All of these materials were commonly used in making false teeth at the time, but wood? Not so much—think of the potential for splinters in the mouth! The idea that George **Washington's** teeth were wooden was popular as long ago as the nineteenth century and may have come from the fact that ivory stained and discolored easily, making those teeth look brown and "woody."

# Ancient sculptures were not plain white.

When we look at Greek and Roman sculptures today in museums, or pictures of them online, they are always clean and plain white. There is something ghostly about them, but also serene. The thing is, they didn't look like this at all at the time. Oh sure, they were carved in plain stone, but then they were painted, often in bright and even outlandish colors. The eyes even had pupils! Researchers know this because they have been able to detect traces of the paint that was once on them but has long since worn off due to the effects of weather or the ravages of time. They were meant to be colorful!

# The Vikings did not have horns on their helmets.

This may surprise you, but there is no evidence anywhere that Vikings wore horned helmets into battle. The confusion came about in the 1870s, during a staging of **Richard Wagner's** Ring Cycle operas, when costume designer **Carl Emil Doepler** envisioned horned helmets for the characters. Though he may have gotten the idea from some obscure, earlier drawings, his particular vision for them took off, and we've been stuck with it in popular culture ever since. The Greeks and Romans did describe horned ceremonial headdresses and helmets worn by the Celts and Germanic peoples, but these were centuries before the Vikings sailed forth, and from different cultures.

# The words "Ye Old" were not used in early English.

Not like that, anyway. In Old and Middle English, there was another letter, **thorn**, which was pronounced as a *th* sound and written like this: þ. So writing "þe old shop" simply meant "the old shop." The letter *y* was used as a substitute in English printing presses (which came from Germany and elsewhere, and didn't have the thorn character). Thorn fell out of use in English by the sixteenth century, but the *y* remained, so when someone later wanted to make something seem "oldie worldie," they wrote "ye," and now we have "ye old" on shop signs and many other places. "Ye" was actually a way of saying "you," but try saying "You Olde Bookshoppe." Just sounds weird, doesn't it?

# Medieval people did not believe that the earth was flat.

Despite what you may have heard, **Christopher Columbus** didn't "prove" the earth was round by sailing to the Caribbean and back. As long ago as the third century BCE, most educated people accepted that the world is a sphere, and that information didn't disappear with the coming of the **Dark Ages** after the fall of Rome. Academics of the Middle Ages spoke of the earth as being round. The idea of a medieval "Flat Earth" delusion seems to have been promoted by seventeenth-century Protestants as an attack on Catholicism, and it became accepted as true in the nineteenth century. The fact that this belief is (weirdly) gaining popularity now would have seemed strange to medieval scholars!

# George Washington did not chop down a cherry tree.

The famed story of George Washington as a six-year-old boy being too honest to lie about his misdeed is a well-known part of American folklore. When his father confronted him, he famously said, "I cannot tell a lie . . . "—impressing his father with his honesty. Except . . . it never happened. The story was invented by an early biographer of Washington's, **Mason Locke Weems**. Weems's biography first appeared in 1800, a year after Washington's death, but the cherry tree tale didn't show up until the fifth edition in 1806. Still, never let the facts get in the way of a good story, and this one certainly took off in the public imagination!

# Mussolini did not make the trains run on time.

It's a well-known joke that sure, **Benito Mussolini** was a fascist dictator, but at least the trains ran on time. It was encouraged by Mussolini himself as a way of proving that his dictatorial system was the most efficient. The thing is, while the Italian train system was in a bit of a state after **World War I**, it had already improved quite a lot by the time Mussolini and his goons came to power. They were only too happy to take credit for something that others had done, of course! Those who lived through his time in power were (later) quick to point out that there was no truth to the legend.

# In the Middle Ages, spices were not mainly used to hide the flavor of rotting meat.

During that time, spices were expensive, imported from lands far away from Europe, such as the Middle East and Asia. They were only affordable to the very wealthy and would not have been wasted on rotting food. Furthermore, meat would have been taken from an animal slaughtered on that day, or perhaps it was smoked and dried for the winter. Either way, people were not sitting down to meals of rotten meat! That doesn't mean the food sanitation was great at the time, of course, just that people wouldn't have wasted their luxuries on food that no one wanted to eat anyway.

# In the Salem Witch Trials, no one was burned at the stake.

The popular image of the witch being burned at the stake haunts our collective imagination. Most regard these people today as innocent victims of fear and superstition. And some of the most famous witches were those accused, tried, and convicted in the little Massachusetts town of Salem in the late seventeenth century. Films, television, and other media have often shown these victims of the **Salem Witch Trials** as being burned at the stake, but the truth is that not one of them was. All but one were hanged, and that unlucky other was pressed to death with rocks. Bonus misconception: they were not all women; of the nineteen people executed, four were men. One of those men was the one pressed to death.

# Thomas Edison did not invent the lightbulb.

**Thomas Edison** was an important inventor in the history of electric devices, to be sure, but the claim that he invented the lightbulb itself is not true. What he did do was to improve on an idea that already existed but wasn't efficient enough. But the idea of the lightbulb itself had been around for most of the nineteenth century, and historians still debate exactly who came up with it first. As early as 1806, an English inventor named **Humphrey Davy** demonstrated a kind of early electric lamp, but it burned out very quickly. Other inventors followed suit and tried making their own. Edison was a latecomer, but his design was the one that lasted.

# Nero did not fiddle while Rome burned.

The image of the mad Roman emperor **Nero** fiddling during the great **fire in Rome** in 64 CE is something that many people still believe: while buildings and people burned, he simply sat and made music. While Nero was indeed an enthusiastic amateur musician (who fancied himself as a professional), there was one problem: the fiddle didn't exist then. The first evidence of bowed instruments in Europe doesn't exist before the eleventh century, a full 1,000 years after Nero. Though such instruments might have existed in Central Asia before then, there's no evidence that they were known or used in ancient Rome. It's said that Nero actually rushed back to the city and tried to help, but soon after, he was more than happy to blame Christians, and build a new palace over the area where homes had burned, so he wasn't a great guy either.

# Suicides did not increase after the stock market crash of October 24, 1929.

There is a popular image of formerly wealthy investors jumping out of windows in high-rises after the **Crash of 1929**, having lost everything they made during the good times that preceded it. This goes along with the belief that there were mass suicides when the **Great Depression** began. But the facts don't show that at all. There were only two recorded incidents of people jumping out of buildings to kill themselves at that time. The number of reported suicides for October and November was lower than at any other time in 1929 and was even lower than at the same time in the previous year.

# The pyramids at Giza were not built by slaves.

Partly informed by biblical stories of **Moses**, there is a widespread belief that the **pyramids at Giza** were built by a merciless pharaoh and that slavery was common in Egypt. But neither of these beliefs is true. While there was indeed much backbreaking and difficult labor involved in erecting these massive monuments at various times, the work was actually carried out mostly by free farmers who worked their off-season. They were paid for their work, ate well, and were housed nearby in barracks on the complex, barracks that still have worker graffiti on the walls. The Greek historian **Herodotus** claimed that the pyramids were built by slaves, but he visited them long after they were built, and was just making things up!

# Napoleon was not short.

The idea that **Napoleon** was small comes from a misunderstanding about how height was measured. The French inch (***pouce***) was longer than the imperial inch, so when he was recorded at being 5'2", it is important to use the French measurements. With those, we get a height of about 5'5," and some say even a bit taller. While this is not "tall" in our modern sense, it was about the average height of most men at the time. He would have been shorter than some and taller than others. But the idea of the **"Napoleon Complex"** is simply not true in his case.

# There is no evidence that Marie Antoinette said, "Let them eat cake."

The image of a callous queen dismissing her hungry subjects' need for bread by telling them to eat cake has long haunted the legacy of **Marie Antoinette**. However, the original quote doesn't even refer to cake, but rather to brioche, a sweet and buttery bread. And the idea of a noble or monarch dismissing the common people's needs goes back way before Marie. The phrase wasn't associated with her until 1843, and may have existed in 1760, when she was only five years old. It's safe to say this was a bit of propaganda put into her mouth. Rather like that cake.

# The forbidden fruit of the book of Genesis is not an apple.

The Bible itself never says what the famed fruit of the **Tree of Knowledge** in the **Garden of Eden** was. In Jewish tradition it has been thought to be many different things, including a fig, a grape, or even wheat. The confusion comes from the Latin translation. In Latin the word *malus* can mean both "evil" and "apple," so some early Christian readers and commentators, reading the Latin, simply assumed that the fruit was an apple. That popular association stuck, even after vernacular translations of the Bible were made, and it has since entered the popular imagination.

# The word "crap" does not derive from Thomas Crapper.

**Thomas Crapper** is known as the inventor of the modern flushing toilet, but he didn't do that. Other attempts were made in earlier times, and he simply made improvements on these efforts. His name seems like the logical origin of the word "crap," but, incredibly, it's just a coincidence. The word actually comes from medieval English and was already in the *Oxford English Dictionary* by the 1840s, long before Crapper set up his new flushing toilet business in the 1860s. As tempting as it is to believe that there must be a connection between the two words, there isn't. Unless, of course, he decided that with a name like that, his career was already predetermined for him . . .

# There is no evidence for a curse on King Tut's tomb.

The idea of a mummy's curse is irresistible: an ancient king cursing anyone who disturbs his bones or tries to steal his treasure. It's the stuff of countless horror movies, and many believe that just such a curse hangs over the tomb of **Tutankhamun**, discovered in 1922. The death of the **Earl of Carnarvon**, who helped finance the venture, in 1923, led to some speculating that sinister forces were at work. Others also seemed to suffer various misfortunes. However, the vast majority of the people connected with opening and excavating the tomb suffered no ill effects at all. **Howard Carter**, who opened the tomb, lived for another sixteen years. A number of tomb guards lived into their seventies. If it was a curse, it took a long time to work, it seems.

# A Roman vomitorium was not a room where people could throw up.

It's an unpleasant image that was meant to not only show disgust, but also to demonstrate the wastefulness of the upper classes in ancient Rome: these wealthy and elites had a room, the vomitorium, set aside where, after feasting and stuffing themselves, they could go, make themselves vomit, and thus have empty stomachs to come back and eat more. Gross. Except these rooms didn't exist. There are a few satirical references in Roman writings, and some outraged Christian descriptions, but Romans believed in proper conduct and honoring their gods. Wasting food this way would have been seen as lacking in morality and squandering resources.

# Julius Caesar was not born by caesarean section.

The very name of the procedure implies that **Julius Caesar** was born by being cut out of his mother's womb. But it's essentially impossible. Before the advent of modern medical procedures, antibiotics, and other surgery, any operations to cut open a woman to remove a fetus would have resulted in the death of the mother and would only have been done as a last resort if she were dying already. Caesar's mother, **Aurelia Cotta**, not only survived the birth but also raised him, and lived until 54 BCE, while he was campaigning in Gaul. None of his early biographers mention this procedure, and while **Pliny the Elder** (23–79 CE) mentions the surgical procedure, it's not linked directly to the dictator, since the name Caesar was common enough already.

# People didn't usually die at about the age of thirty during the Middle Ages.

This is a misunderstanding of the term "average age." The average is the total sum divided by the number of units in a group. So, the average of the numbers 0 and 60 is 30 (0 + 60 ÷ 2 = 30). When looking at life spans in the Middle Ages, one must account for the very high rates of infant and child mortality, which were probably over 50 percent. So, when weighing that death rate against longer life spans, the average will bring that number down. But the reality is that during the Middle Ages and later periods, if you survived to the age of twenty-one, you had a decent chance of making it to sixty years old.

# King Canute did not expect the tide to retreat.

The story tells of the vain **King Canute**, who ruled England in the early eleventh century and who went down to a bank on the River Thames and, holding out his hand, commanded the tide to recede and not to fill in his land. The tide, of course, took no notice of him and kept on rising, showing his foolishness and the foolishness of any who think they can stand against nature, no matter what their social status is. Except the story doesn't end there: in the original account, as the tide keeps coming in, Canute said that this illustrated how worldly power was trivial, and that only God had true power. It was actually meant to show his humility and be a teaching moment for his courtiers, but the second half of the story got dropped. In any case, this story only first appeared about one century later, so it likely never happened at all.

# There is no proof that the iron maiden existed in the Middle Ages.

The **iron maiden** is a hideous torture/execution device depicted in many movies and films about the Middle Ages: a spiked coffin into which victims were forced and then the lid closed. The spikes were short enough that they wouldn't kill someone immediately. It was an absolutely ghastly way to die a painful death, and the epitome of medieval superstition and cruelty. But there's no evidence of it before the eighteenth century; no surviving versions, no accounts of its use as a torture, nothing. While something like it may have existed in ancient Rome, even there it may be a later idea projected back onto the age. The medieval iron maiden seems to be one of those eighteenth-century falsehoods created to show how barbaric the time was.

# Columbus did not discover the Americas.

The idea of the Americas being discovered by anyone in Europe is, of course, laughable now, but the story was long taught to schoolchildren. Christopher Columbus also supposedly proved the world was round (in fact, this was well known at the time, as mentioned above). First of all, the American Indians who crossed the Bering Strait thousands of years ago were the true discoverers of the northern and southern American continents. Columbus only landed in the Caribbean islands. Not the continent. And even by Columbus's time, another European had already sailed into North America about five hundred years earlier: the Icelander Leif Erikson, who probably sailed as far as Newfoundland in Canada. Columbus was a latecomer by comparison.

# Chastity belts probably never existed in the Middle Ages.

The idea of a jealous father or husband locking up wives and daughters in these bizarre contraptions to make sure that they don't stray while said man is gone seems offensive and ridiculous to modern sensibilities, and one more jab at the intolerant and awful Middle Ages. The thing is, the idea of the **chastity belt** is almost certainly another later invention that has no basis in historical fact. They are mentioned in satirical texts, along with devices for making one invisible, but no one seems to have taken them seriously, until the eighteenth and nineteenth centuries, when some men had them made; these can be found in museums.

# The Aztecs did not mistake Hernán Cortés and his men for gods.

The idea that the mighty **Aztec Empire** was brought down by a much smaller number of Spanish explorers and colonizers has led to many historians looking for explanations. One of these is that the Aztecs saw **Hernán Cortés** and his men as divine beings, and so allowed themselves to be run down and conquered, simply because they didn't resist these newcomers. In fact, Cortés was able to enlist the help of many smaller groups of indigenous peoples who weren't all that thrilled with being ruled by the Aztecs and paying their crippling tax rates (not mention their human sacrifices). Cortés never wrote that he was welcomed as a god. It was only several decades later that the story appeared, possibly created by the remaining Aztec people to justify to themselves why they had lost their empire.

# Marco Polo did not bring back pasta from China.

It seems perfectly logical. China invented noodles, and **pasta** is a staple of Italian cooking. Therefore, **Marco Polo**, an Italian, must have brought back noodles from China, and accidentally started a whole new branch of Italian cuisine. But he didn't. He mentions certain types of noodles but from the point of view of a kind of food he already knows about. An account by an Arab traveler over a century earlier already talks about a type of food in Sicily made from flour that is shaped like strings . . . sounds a lot like pasta! Certain kinds of noodles were already known in the Middle East (especially Persia), and could easily have already been traded and eaten in Italy in Marco Polo's time.

# Isaac Newton never said that an apple hit him on the head.

It is one of the most beloved scenes in the history of science. Isaac Newton, while sitting under an apple tree, is hit on the head by an apple falling out of it. He immediately begins to wonder why things fall down instead of falling up. From this observation, he works out his theory of gravity, changing the scientific world forever. The thing is, it didn't quite happen that way. He did wonder why objects fall down instead of some other direction, and he did mention that he observed the falling of apples, but there's no evidence that one ever hit him on the head. That story seems to be a charming later invention.

# The Declaration of Independence was not signed on July 4, 1776.

It's at the heart of what so many believe about American history: The **Founding Fathers** sat in a room and signed the **Declaration of Independence** on July 4, 1776, declaring that the colonies were now independent of Britain. It's a potent image that goes with the national identity. But it didn't really happen that way. The Founders actually declared independence from Britain on July 2, 1776, and formalized the document on July 4. But it wasn't actually signed until August 2, 1776.

# Cinco de Mayo is not Mexico's Independence Day.

Cinco de Mayo is widely thought of as a Mexican Independence Day celebration, mostly by those of non-Hispanic origins, who like to spend the day drinking beer and eating Mexican food (it's a rather minor holiday in Mexico, by contrast). In fact, the day celebrates a victory on May 5, 1862, when the Mexican army defeated the French army at the **Battle of Puebla** during the **Franco-Mexican War**. Mexico's actual Independence Day is September 16.

# The Chicago Fire of 1871 was not caused by Mrs. O'Leary's cow kicking over a lantern.

The terrible fire that ravaged Chicago in 1871 is thought by many to have had a very humble (and silly) beginning: when a cow belonging to one Catherine O'Leary accidentally kicked over a lit lantern while she milked it; the fire quickly spread. O'Leary and her husband were Irish Catholic immigrants, and already faced considerable prejudice in their new home, so this story was one more way of piling on the hatred. While the fire may have started in their barn, no one would have been milking a cow after 9:00 p.m., so Catherine probably had nothing to do with it. Someone else may have been using the barn to smoke, gamble, etc., and from that, the fire started and spread.

# Franklin D. Roosevelt probably did not have polio.

It has long been believed that President Franklin D. Roosevelt, who spent much of his adult life in a wheelchair, was stricken with polio, making him paralyzed from the waist down. In the summer of 1921, he came down with fever, chills, and various other symptoms, eventually losing the use of his legs. It was assumed that polio, a scourge of the outdoors in summer months, was the cause. But more recent research shows that his symptoms are more consistent with Guillain–Barré syndrome, an autoimmune disorder that can be triggered by infections and other outside causes.

# Rosa Parks was not sitting at the front of the bus when she refused to move.

**Rosa Parks** did not defiantly sit in the "white section" of the bus on that fateful day of December 1, 1955, when she was arrested. She was in fact seated in the first row of the "Black section" of the bus, but it was nevertheless required that Black people give up their seats if white people wanted them to do so. She was asked to stand up and refused. She also said that she did not refuse because she was tired, merely "tired of giving in."

# Al Gore never said that he invented the internet.

This little story was a popular jab at **Al Gore** in the 2000 presidential election, but it's not what he really said. His exact words were: "During my service in the United States Congress, I took the initiative in creating the **internet**. I took the initiative in moving forward a whole range of initiatives that have proven to be important to our country's economic growth and environmental protection . . . " In other words, he helped craft legislation that led to the spread and usefulness of the internet, among other things. He didn't invent it.

# Benjamin Franklin did not discover electricity.

The popular image of **Benjamin Franklin** flying his kite in a thunderstorm and it being hit by lightning, thus leading to the "discovery" of electricity, is another of those beloved tales of American folklore. But he didn't really "discover" anything. Electricity had been known long before that June 1752 day. What Franklin was able to show was a connection between electricity and lightning. Also, his kite was not struck by lightning; he probably would have died if it had been. Rather, it picked up electrical charge from the thunderstorm. And he was not the first to do it; a Frenchman named **Thomas-François Dalibard** showed the relationship only a month before Franklin did.

# The "Dark Ages" were not a thing.

The **Dark Ages** is a popular term for the supposed "darkness" of the time between the fall of the **Roman Empire** in the fifth century and the **Renaissance** in Europe, beginning around 1400. The era was dismissed as a time of barbarity and superstition, a gap between the ancient greatness of the Greco-Roman world and the greatness of the "modern" world. The "Dark Ages" could also refer to the centuries between Rome's fall and, say, **William the Conqueror** in 1066, because, due to a lack of written records in many areas, historians were often "in the dark" about what happened. In general, though, it's no longer used. The terms "early Middle Ages" and "early medieval period" are now more preferred.

# Hitler was not a vegetarian.

Not completely, anyway. Before the war, **Adolf Hitler** was known for consuming a variety of meat products. He does seem to have curtailed his diet and eliminated most meat during **World War II**, but not all. Until at least 1942, he remained fond of *leberknödl*, or liver dumpling, for example, and had no problem taking various experimental medicines that contained many kinds of animal products and extracts. Like so much about **Nazi** propaganda, his image as a non-meat-eater was fostered to show his discipline and "purity," but behind the scenes he didn't always practice what he preached.

# Millions were not killed in the European witch trials.

It was a shameful time in European history, when innocents were accused of being witches and dragged into courts, where they were often tortured and then sentenced to be burned or hanged or executed in some other appalling way. These horrid trials did indeed happen, and many innocent victims died at the hands of cruel inquisitors and greedy neighbors who wanted their land, but the numbers are a lot more difficult to prove. For a long time, the number nine million was floated around with authority, but this seems to have originated at a witchcraft museum in England and has no basis in fact. The actual number is now estimated to be around 100,000 over three centuries (fifteenth through seventeenth), an appalling amount, to be sure, but far from the millions once claimed. And of that number, up to one-quarter might have been men.

# The word "f—ck" does not come from "Fornication Under Consent of the King."

The idea of this word coming from an acronym seems appealing at first, but it's just not true. Some sources have claimed that a sign with these words was placed over English brothels (meaning they were legal and licensed), or that people had to get the king's permission to have a child, both of which are nonsense. Other sources have said that it was an acronym for the phrase, "For Unlawful Carnal Knowledge," a legal charge. The fact is, everyone's favorite curse word came from other languages, such as the Middle Dutch *fokken*, "to thrust, to copulate with," and the Norwegian *fukka*, "to copulate." Oh, and there is also the wonderfully named John le Fucker, cited in a manuscript from the year 1250.

# Mark Twain never said, "The coldest winter I ever spent was a summer in San Francisco."

**Mark Twain** is credited with all sorts of wonderful witticisms, some of which are his, and many that are not. Unfortunately, this clever little line, which just about everyone knows (especially tour guides in San Francisco!), was never said by the great writer. A search of his writings reveals no trace of it, though he did make other remarks about the weather, including one about Paris being cold in summertime.

# A bullet did not cause a woman during the American Civil War to become pregnant.

This too-weird-to-be-true story really is. It's a popular tale in the "believe it or not" circles, which says that a bullet grazed the scrotum of a soldier (ouch!) and lodged in the uterus of a Virginia woman nearby. It was enough to impregnate her, and she not only survived, but nine months later, gave birth to a healthy baby boy. The story appeared in *The American Medical Weekly* way back in 1874, and though it was later debunked as a hoax, this hasn't stopped it from spreading, urban legend–style, until it has become a popular piece of American folklore. But it never happened.

# Voltaire didn't say, "I disapprove of what you say, but I will defend to the death your right to say it."

Another famous quote, this one seems to be a hallmark of eighteenth-century **Enlightenment** thought, and something that free-speech advocates love to cite to show how we don't have to agree on everything, but we must respect the rights of others to speak freely. However, **Voltaire** never said it. It was invented by a biographer of Voltaire, **Evelyn Beatrice Hall**, who created it for her biography of him, *The Friends of Voltaire*, in 1906. She even admitted that she made it up as an expression of his beliefs. And then it got attributed to the man himself.

# Pilgrims did not wear buckles on their hats.

In popular imagination (and in most Thanksgiving pictures), the **pilgrims** at the first **Thanksgiving** wore all black and had those conical hats with wide brims and distinct square buckles on them as part of the hatband. In reality, black was formal wear even then, and the early **Puritan** settlers wore a variety of colors in their clothing. Their hats were conical, but never had buckles. Those kinds of buckles were more of an upper-class thing that only became fashionable later in the seventeenth century, and then mainly as parts of belts, just as you might expect.

# John F. Kennedy did not say, "I am a jelly donut" in 1963.

This is another story that people like to laugh about: When President **John F. Kennedy** spoke in Berlin in 1963, he uttered the famous phrase: *Ich bin ein Berliner*, which means "I am a Berliner." The problem was, some people assumed that this was grammatically incorrect, and that he should have said *Ich bin Berliner*, because the way he said it made it seem like he was referring to "a" Berliner, more properly known as a *Berliner Pfannkuchen*, a type of jelly-filled pasty. Often, this treat is just called a "Berliner." So yes, technically he said that, but saying either *Ich bin ein Berliner* or *Ich bin Berliner* can both mean one is of Berlin, just as we might say, "I am American," or "I am an American."

# Van Gogh may or may not have cut off his ear.

Most people have heard the story of **Vincent van Gogh**, the brilliant painter but tormented genius who in a fit cut off his ear and presented it to a woman he admired. The story is kind-of, sort-of true, but there's more to it than that. On December 23, 1888, after confronting his fellow painter **Paul Gauguin**, van Gogh was reported to have slashed his ear off and then presented it wrapped up to a woman at a local brothel. Most assume it was the whole ear, but more recently, doubt has been cast on this. Some think it was only a small portion of the earlobe, while others point out conflicting reports from witnesses and the doctor about just how much of the ear he managed to take off. Some said very little; some said a lot. So, we don't know, but it probably wasn't the whole ear. If that was the case, he would likely have bled to death.

# P. T. Barnum never said, "There's a sucker born every minute."

It's such a famous phrase, and everyone knows that showman **P. T. Barnum** said it, right? It turns out he didn't. One of his biographers could find no trace of the phrase, and it is unclear if the word "sucker" was even widely used in that insulting way at the time. Barnum tended to be very grateful for his many customers and wouldn't have made fun of them. The phrase definitely existed at a later date, though, especially in casinos and other betting environments, where it would make more sense.

# Lady Godiva probably didn't ride naked.

The famed story of **Lady Godiva** says that she was disturbed by her husband's high taxes on the people of the English town of **Coventry**. He promised to lower taxes if she rode on a horse, naked, through the town. She asked all the people in town to remain indoors and close their curtains, and then she indeed made the ride. But one man, Tom, couldn't resist a glance, earning the name **Peeping Tom**. Her husband gave in and lowered their taxes. Except it never happened. **Lady Godgifu** was an eleventh-century noblewoman, wife of **Leofric**, the Earl of Mercia. She was deeply pious and would never have agreed to anything like this. Plus, the story doesn't appear for over two hundred years after she lived. And Coventry at the time was more like a simple village than a bustling town. It's just another (not so) urban legend!

# Sir Walter Raleigh didn't put down his cloak for Queen Elizabeth I.

A famous story of chivalry: **Sir Walter Raleigh** was said to have laid his cloak over a muddy puddle so that **Queen Elizabeth I** could step on it and not get her royal feet wet. But the story was invented in the seventeenth century, probably by historian **Thomas Fuller**, and embellished in **Sir Walter Scott**'s 1821 work *Kenilworth*. Raleigh was indeed a favorite of the queen's in the 1580s, but later fell out of favor for romancing one of Elizabeth's maids of honor. By then, laying a cloak down for her wouldn't have made any difference!

# Paul Revere did not shout "The British are coming!" on his night ride.

Everyone knows about **Paul Revere**'s famous ride, to warn the colonists of an impending invasion of British troops. The thing is, in his time, the colonists still considered themselves British, so yelling that they were coming would have made no sense at all. It would be like riding through the countryside of Massachusetts today yelling, "The Americans are coming!" He did make a nighttime ride to warn colonists about the troops, but he was one of dozens of other riders, and their mission depended on secrecy. In fact, he was captured by the British and later released after being questioned.

# Cowboys did not wear cowboy hats.

The image of **cowboys** in the **Old West** is one that inhabits popular imagination, and one of the most enduring parts of that image is the broad-brimmed **Stetson** hat. This hat is still popular in various places through the United States today. The thing is, "real" cowboys didn't wear this kind of hat. They preferred the **bowler** or derby hat. Cowboys like Bat Masterson, **Butch Cassidy**, and the **Sundance Kid** are all seen in photos wearing derby hats. Larger hats would not have stayed on as easily and would have made them easier targets. The Stetson was available from the 1860s but didn't really become more popular until the end of the nineteenth century, when the "classic age" of the cowboy was coming to an end.

# Henry VIII did not divorce his wives.

Well, of course he executed two of them, one died in childbirth, and one outlived him, but what about the other two? It's commonly known that **Henry VIII** was unhappy with the failure of his first wife, **Katherine of Aragon**, to produce a male heir. He was later unimpressed with his fourth wife, **Anne of Cleves**. But in both cases, he did not divorce them; he had the marriages annulled. This meant that, legally speaking, they never happened to begin with. Getting an actual divorce approved by the church was almost impossible in those days, one of the main reasons Henry VIII broke with the **Roman Catholic Church** and set up his own **Church of England**.

# The "Wild West" wasn't all that wild.

Shoot-outs, bank robberies, outlaws, and more . . . danger and adventure in the American West are the stuff of legends and classic movies. But these ideas are largely exaggerated. In many towns, it was illegal to carry guns openly (they often had to be surrendered to the sheriff). Only a handful of bank robberies are recorded (these crimes were way more common in big cities back east), and quick-draw gunfights/duels are mostly exciting fiction. At the end of the 1870s, the town of **Palisade**, Nevada, decided to stage some gunfights and robberies for the entertainment of people passing through, and this helped to contribute to the Wild West legend, but, in general, these frontier towns were pretty uneventful and even boring.

# CHAPTER 2:
## Science

**Scientific literacy seems to be in decline these days,** with a disturbing and increasing number of people willing to believe outrageous things that have no basis in fact. Acceptance of scientific findings seems to come and go in cycles, and while the deniers are louder than they ever have been, science continues to provide an essential light in the dark for understanding our immensely complex world and universe. This chapter looks at some widely believed misconceptions about all kinds of science and technology topics. Read through these when you feel like you need a dose of fascinating reality!

# Lightning can indeed strike in the same place twice.

The popular old folk belief that **lightning** will only ever strike a place once is just that: a misconception that's not true. Meteorologists and weather-watchers have always known this and can easily show in storm footage that anything can be struck more than once. Where a site is hit has nothing to do with whether or not lightning will strike it again. Some places may be struck multiple times during one storm, or lightning might indeed strike a place once and then not again for years, if ever.

# Meteors are not on fire when they reach the earth.

Disaster movies always like to show **meteors** as flaming blocks of rock streaking through the sky, but this is only partly correct. Any object floating through space will be incredibly cold, even frozen. The glow that we see on a meteor comes from its hitting Earth's atmosphere, thus causing friction and heat. This heat will indeed burn off some of the outer layer of a rock, but it's not really "on fire" in the way we might think. It's difficult to know if meteors are still hot when they hit the surface, because it's very difficult to get to a site of a meteor impact right away. But many scientists believe that smaller rocks especially won't be warm at all when they crash-land.

# There are more than just three states of matter.

We've heard it said that matter can exist in three states: solid, liquid, and gas. Water is a liquid, nitrogen is a gas, and a rock is a solid. But there are other states as well. The most common form of matter in the universe is actually plasma, which is an ionized gas. This is a gas in which there is sufficient heat and energy to strip away electrons from atoms, creating a "soup" of positively charged particles, called ions, and negatively charged particles, called electrons. Stars, including our own sun, are made of plasma.

# Toilet flushes do not spin in the opposite direction in the Southern Hemisphere.

This is a long-held but incorrect belief. It does have some truth, though. The earth is subject to the **Coriolis effect**, an inertial force that will determine how hurricanes spin, for example: counterclockwise in the Northern Hemisphere and clockwise in the Southern Hemisphere. While this force exists, it has no real effect on toilets, bathtubs, etc. The way your toilet drains has far more to do with how it is designed, and the direction the water pours into the bowl. So, you can't simply tell which hemisphere you're in by looking at your flushing toilet bowl!

# We have more than five senses.

We've always heard that we have five senses: sight, hearing, touch, taste, and smell. But science now recognizes that there may be as many as eighteen or more. Some of the others include: **Proprioception** (the ability to tell where your body parts are in space and in relation to other body parts), **Nociception** (the ability to feel pain), **Equilibrioception** (the ability to keep one's balance), vestibular senses (telling up from down and side to side), **Chronoception** (the ability to sense the passage of time), and even hunger and thirst!

# Human beings did not evolve from apes (we share a common ancestor).

An argument that some try to use against evolution is: "If we evolved from apes, why are there still apes now?" It's a silly question that contains a basic misunderstanding about how evolution works. No, we did not evolve from gorillas, chimps, or any other apes. Humans, like those species, are primates, and every variety of human, along with the apes, evolved from a common ancestor. We simply branched off into different family trees over millions of years.

# Humans use more than 10 percent of their brains.

This weird fallacy has been around for a while. It may have originated with Harvard psychologist **William James**, who in 1907 wrote that "we are making use of only a small part of our possible mental and physical resources." But he wasn't talking about using only 10 percent of our brains; he was referring to the fact that we can get too accustomed to our surroundings and not engage with them fully. **Positron Emission Tomography (PET)** scans that measure brain activity show clearly that all parts of the brain are lighting up and active, even during sleep.

# A penny dropped from a tall building will not kill anyone.

Another mistaken belief: if you drop a penny off the **Empire State Building** and it hits someone, it will be traveling at enough of a velocity to kill that person. It's simply too light and would actually probably flutter to the ground, more like a leaf. It would achieve its maximum velocity after falling about fifty feet and would then only fall at about twenty-five mph. It might annoy you if you got hit, but nothing more.

# Albert Einstein did not fail math.

This belief is pretty common in some circles and may continue to be popular as a way of saying that doing well or poorly in school is not always an indication of future achievements and success. If **Albert Einstein** couldn't handle math, then how bad can the rest of us be? Well, here's the bad news. Not only did he not flunk math, but also he seemed to excel at it. He wrote, "Before I was fifteen, I had mastered differential and integral calculus." He did later drop out of school, so there's that, but it wasn't because he couldn't deal with math!

# The Great Wall of China is not the only human-made object visible from space.

In fact, the **Great Wall of China** is often invisible itself, except in low-Earth orbit. This is because it's made of the same materials as its surroundings. Many astronauts have been unable to locate it. And it's most definitely not visible from the moon. The most visible signs of human structure are cities, especially at night, when the lights are on.

# You can balance an egg any day of the year, not just at the spring equinox.

An old wives' tale says that you can only balance an egg longwise on the **spring equinox**, because on that date, the earth is in a special gravitational relationship to the sun that allows for it. This seems weird and unbelievable, but people test it out every year. Here's the thing: you can balance an egg on its bigger end longwise on any day of the year, if you have the right egg and keep on trying. It has much more to do with the shape and position of the yolk than anything else.

# Apple computers (Macs) are not immune to computer viruses.

Sorry, **Mac** fans! Often, you'll see warnings of new viruses go around, and owners of Macs will smugly chime in that they have a Mac, and so don't need to worry about it. Well, that's just not true. What is true is that far more viruses and Trojans are created for **PCs**, simply because PCs are still far more widely used. But there have been and still are some nasty viruses out there designed for Macs, and your beloved laptop can still get infected. So, keep your antivirus software up to date, no matter what kind of computer you have. Don't be vulnerable—be smart!

# Human blood is not blue.

There is a belief that human blood is actually blue but turns red when it oxygen touches it. This is why you bleed red. But it's nonsense; blood is always red. Our blood has a protein called **hemoglobin**, which has a red-colored compound, **heme**, which has an iron atom. Blood is darker red in the body, but still red. So why are our veins blue? It has to do with the light that penetrates our skin. Blue light does not get as far in and is reflected back outward, making it look like our veins might be blue. That's all.

# Being in a vacuum (such as space) will not make a human body explode.

It's a trope of some science fiction and horror films: a person is ejected into space (or a cabin on a spaceship depressurizes), they writhe in pain, and then splatter all over the place. Yuck. But that doesn't happen. What does happen isn't all that much better, though. In the vacuum of space, there is not the atmospheric pressure that our bodies are accustomed to. If someone did not immediately exhale any remaining air in their lungs, said lungs would likely rupture in the pressure differential, causing an immediate and painful death. Just something to keep in mind.

# Stretching before or after exercise does not reduce soreness.

Stretching can be useful in certain circumstances, but it doesn't have much to do with reducing how sore you feel after a workout or exercise routine. Various studied have been conducted that have shown that the effects of stretching to reduce pain and soreness are minimal at best. And it didn't seem to matter if this was before or after a workout. So, if you think stretching out your legs is going to help you not be sore after that five-mile run, it's probably going to do very little.

# Urine is not sterile.

This has been promoted by some survivalists as a way of staying alive (i.e., you can drink your own urine to hydrate if you have to, because urine is sterile). But it's not. To be "sterile" would mean that it must be free of any bacteria or other substances. And urine contains plenty of those, even in healthy adults. Our bladders have all kinds of necessary bacteria to function, and some of these will be peed out. Bonus misconception: do not pee on a jellyfish sting! It might make it hurt even more!

# Tastes are not limited to certain areas of your tongue.

It was long thought that we can only taste certain tastes on specific areas of our tongues: salty on the tip and sides, sweet in the middle and tip, sour at the sides, and bitter in the back. But this so-called tongue map, though long promoted, even in textbooks, is incorrect. It came from a 1901 study by German scientist **David Hänig** that tried to map out areas of sensitivity on the tongue. And while it's true that there are different regions with different taste sensitivities, all parts of the tongue are capable of tasting all flavors in different amounts. And speaking of flavors . . .

# There are more than four flavors.

We long ago learned that there are four basic tastes: salty, sweet, sour, and bitter. Everything we eat will be one of these or some combination. But there's another flavor that is present in many foods, now known by its Japanese name, **umami**. Umami is technically known as glutamate, a kind of amino acid. It is a savory flavor, as opposed to a salty one, and can be found in things like mushrooms and tomatoes. A case is now being made for a sixth flavor, oleogustus (say that three times fast!), which is a fatty flavor.

# Shaving does not make hair grow back thicker.

This is an old belief. But shaving doesn't affect the thickness of hairs, or the speed at which they grow. A shaved hair is going to have a blunt tip and is going to feel coarser because of it. This is most noticeable when the hair is starting to pop out of the skin again and feels rough. But it's not because it's getting thicker. If it were allowed to grow out, it would be the same as all the other hairs around it.

# Hair and nails do not continue to grow after death.

This creepy misconception has been around for a long time. It's unsettling to think that a corpse may keep right on growing hair after a person has died, maybe even for weeks, but that's not what's happening. After death, the skin will dehydrate and the soft tissues will begin to shrink, so what's happening is that the skin is retracting, showing more of the hair that was always there, just hidden underneath the skin. The same is true for nails. Neither hair nor nails are subject to this shrinkage, so it might look like they've grown out a bit.

# Cracking your knuckles will not cause arthritis.

This one is in the same category as "if you cross your eyes too much, they'll get stuck that way." Joints generally crack not from anything to do with the bones, but rather from nitrogen gas being pulled into the joint; it's more like popping a bubble. And cracking them definitely doesn't cause arthritis. In general, cracking your knuckles is harmless (except it might gross out some people!), unless there's pain when you do it, in which case, don't! Seek the advice of a medical professional.

# Vitamin C does not prevent colds.

This one has been around for a very long time. Studies have shown that, except in the case of people who are extremely active, taking large doses of **vitamin C** does little to nothing to prevent colds. It can be somewhat helpful if you already have a cold, but the benefits are not huge, to be honest. Research suggests that zinc may be more effective at reducing the severity and duration of a cold. Now, we need vitamin C, of course, and as long as you're not ingesting megadoses, it's good for you, but don't rely on it when cold season comes around.

# Hansen's disease (leprosy) is actually not a very contagious disease.

Lepers have been social outcasts going back to biblical times and before. Because of the horrible effects the disease has on the skin and body if left untreated, lepers have long been shunned by society and forced to live in groups or colonies on their own. The thing is, leprosy is caused by a bacterial infection, and it's surprisingly difficult to catch, unless one is in contact with an untreated person for longer periods of time. It can be transmitted by coughing and sneezing, but it's nowhere near as contagious as, say, a common cold.

# Rust does not cause tetanus.

As children most of us were probably told to be careful around rusty nails, old machinery, or anything that was metal and rusted. We could risk getting **tetanus** that way. And while it's true that old metal objects can transmit the infection, rust has nothing to do with it. Tetanus is caused by bacteria, and while it can indeed be present on rusty old metal objects, there's no guarantee that it's there. Also, it's a much bigger risk if you receive a puncture wound, such as stepping on a nail, allowing the bacteria to enter deeply into your body. A scratch is far less likely to transmit the infection. In any case, make sure you keep up to date on your tetanus shot!

# Cold weather does not cause colds.

Do you remember your mother saying something like, "Dress warm, you don't want to catch cold!" Well, sorry to say, cold weather doesn't cause colds. Colds are viruses, and there are several reasons why you might be more prone to catching them in the winter. Some viruses live better in cooler temperatures and are more likely to stay on surfaces longer. Also, in winter, we tend to spend more time inside with others, and if someone has been out and picked up a cold, they're more likely to spread it around once they're inside. Getting overly chilled can suppress your immune system, however, making you potentially more vulnerable, so it's still a good idea to bundle up!

# Antibiotics are useless against viruses.

**Antibiotics** are one of the miracles of twentieth-century medicine. With the discovery of how to treat bacteria-caused diseases, countless lives have been saved. But bacteria are clever little organisms that are constantly evolving to find new ways to survive. Antibiotic-resistant strains are becoming an increasing problem, and the overprescribing of antibiotics is one reason for this. People think they need antibiotics for colds and flu, and sometimes doctors prescribe them, or people take old ones they have lying around. But viruses are not bacteria, and antibiotics have no effect on them. You're not only talking something that won't work, but you could also be weakening your own resistance, as well as suffering antibiotic side effects that you don't need. Take them for bacterial infections only.

# Schizophrenia is not a multiple personality disorder.

You may have heard about someone having a "split personality" or "multiple identities," and also heard them referred to as being schizophrenic, but in reality, they are not the same thing. People with **dissociative identity disorder** are the ones who may exhibit multiple personalities, while those with **schizophrenia** will have psychotic episodes, including hallucinations, hearing voices, and delusions (believing in things which have no basis in reality). While both are serious conditions that require medication and treatment, they are not the same.

# The ozone layer does not cause climate change.

The **ozone layer** is an essential component of our atmosphere that shields the earth from harmful **ultraviolet radiation (UV)** emitted by the sun. Decades ago, we discovered that certain chemicals were punching a hole in the ozone layer over Antarctica, which caused widespread alarm. Measures were taken to help repair it (such as banning these chemicals), but some extra UV still gets through, though not nearly enough to cause the changes in temperature that are now being recorded. Furthermore, ozone is itself a **greenhouse gas**, so the layer's thinning has made the Southern Hemisphere actually a bit colder, affecting atmospheric circulation. But it's not driving climate change.

# Einstein never said, "Insanity is doing the same thing over and over again and expecting different results."

It's a great quote, one that we like to apply to all kinds of situations, so it seems only logical that one of the greatest minds of the twentieth century must have said it, right? Unfortunately, **Albert Einstein** didn't say it. This exact quote seems to have originated in some **Alcoholics Anonymous** literature form the early 1980s, though the concept was discussed in psychology starting in the late nineteenth century, usually in a derogatory manner about the mentally ill.

# Seasons are not caused by the earth's proximity to the sun.

The earth's orbit around the sun is elliptical, meaning that it's not a perfect circle. Sometimes we are closer to the sun, and sometimes father away, depending on where we are in the year. But this proximity has nothing to do with our seasons. Seasons happen because of the **axial tilt**. The earth rotates on an axis that is tilted at about 23.4 degrees, meaning that different parts of the globe receive different amounts of the sun's energies at different times of the year, again depending on where we are in our position around the sun. It's why we have summer in the Northern hemisphere when it's winter in the Southern hemisphere, and vice versa.

# Waking up a sleepwalker will not harm them.

It was long thought that one should never wake up a sleepwalker. The sensation of being woken up from sleep while standing, in an unfamiliar place would be too shocking. They might suffer a heart attack, a stroke, or some other terrible fate—or so the theory went. The good news is that this is not true. The person might be disoriented and even frightened, but there's no evidence at all that waking someone up while they are walking causes any harm. In fact, it might prevent them from accidentally hurting themselves by bumping into something, falling down a flight of stairs, etc.

# Dairy does not increase mucus.

There's a belief that one shouldn't drink milk or other thick drinks when one has a head cold, since it will cause the body to produce more phlegm and make the sufferer even more miserable. It seems to make sense, since milk is much thicker than water. While it may make the phlegm you have feel a bit thicker as it drips down the back or your throat (ew!), it does not actually cause your body to produce more. It's better to stick with broths and thinner drinks when sick, simply because they'll probably make you feel better, but milk isn't going to make your cold symptoms worse.

# Men do not think about sex every seven seconds.

#notallmen, anyway! Seriously, if this were true, it would work out to about 514 times an hour, which seems a bit ridiculous! Various studies have tried experiments to determine a more realistic number, but the problem is that they are contaminated by the so-called **white bear problem**: tell someone not to think of a white bear, and they'll start thinking about it, or vice versa. If people know they are measuring how often they think about sex, it stands to reason they will either think of it more, or try to put it out of their minds, either way skewing the results. Even so, studies have suggested lower numbers like nineteen times a day, or even only seven times. These seem more realistic, at least!

# The earth is not a perfect sphere.

Ah, our globe! Models of the earth (i.e., tilted globes that spin) are still popular household and school items and are by far the most accurate maps that we have for the actual size of the continents and oceans. The only problem is, they're presented as perfect, ball-shaped spheres, and the actual Earth isn't shaped like that. Not quite, anyway. Since mass is unevenly placed around the world, with different continents and oceans, it's actually bumpier. Also, since the planet spins, it is slightly flatter at the poles and bulges a bit at the equator. But, to be fair, all of this would be very hard to put on a small globe!

# A coin flip is not always 50/50.

It turns out that a coin toss may not always be the fairest way of deciding something. Due to complex things like math and physics, a coin slightly favors the side that's facing up when the coin is tossed, so the odds are actually a bit closer to 51/49. A spinning US penny, on the other hand, will tend to favor the tails side about 80 percent of the time, because the heads side is a bit heavier. Keep that last bit to yourselves if you want to impress people with your "knowledge" of how the coin will fall!

# Pythagoras did not discover the Pythagorean Theorem.

**Pythagoras of Samos** (ca. 570–ca. 495 BCE) has long been associated with the geometry theorem that bears his name; you might remember it from high school, but probably want to forget it, so we'll spare you the recap here. In fact, the idea behind it was already known by the Babylonians at least 1,200 years earlier. Some have suggested that Pythagoras might have constructed a mathematical proof for the **Pythagorean Theorem**, but his teachings tended to focus on the sacredness of numbers; there would have been no need to "prove" anything about them. The attribution of the theorem to Pythagoras seems to have come along several centuries later.

# Leaving your phone plugged in after it is fully charged does not damage the battery.

This has been a belief among cell phone users for years. People have long warned not to leave one's cell phone plugged in overnight, since charging a battery that's already fully charged will diminish the battery's capacity, or damage it somehow. But these kinds of batteries use what are known as charging cycles, and once a battery is charged up, it won't take in any more current until it is drained and needs to start the next cycle. Modern cell phone batteries are designed this way. So, if you do forget and leave your phone plugged in for a long time after it's charged, it won't do any damage to the battery or the phone.

# The sun is not a yellow star.

Our sun can be seen as many different colors throughout the day. Most notably, it can give off red light at sunrise or sunset. Technically, the sun is classified as a **yellow dwarf star**, which makes it different from a **red dwarf** star and other kinds of stars. But that doesn't mean that our sun is yellow, even if it is often shown that way in pictures. The sun is actually white when seen from space. It's our atmosphere that gives it different colors in different conditions.

# The moon is only one factor in the tides.

We all know that the moon controls the tides. Yes, to a point. Earth's satellite is quite large relative to our planet, and so it's only logical that its own gravity, though much less than Earth's, would have an effect on our planet in many ways. It generates something called the **tidal force**, which causes the water in the oceans to literally bulge out toward the moon. These bulges are responsible for high and low tides. But the sun also exerts some control over the tides, as do Earth conditions like weather systems (high and low pressure) and powerful winds. So, the moon doesn't do the job all by itself!

# The North Star (Polaris) is not the brightest star in the sky.

The **North Star** points to true north, and is easily findable at night, but that doesn't make it the brightest star in the night sky. In the Southern hemisphere, it's mostly unseen. The brightest nighttime star is the **Dog Star Sirius**, and, after that, **Canopus**. The North Star is actually only about the fiftieth brightest star in the sky. And if we want to get pedantic, the brightest star in the sky is our very own sun!

# There is no "dark side of the moon."

We always see the same side of the moon facing us, because the moon is tidally locked with Earth. But there is no **"dark side,"** just a side that we don't see. During the course of the moon's orbit around Earth and its cycle from waxing to waning, the far side of the moon will definitely be bathed in the sun's light, just as all of the moon will be "dark" during the new moon phase. So, while it's true that there's a side to the moon that we only ever see in photographs, it's not dark. Sorry, Pink Floyd.

# A scientific theory is not a guess.

In science, a theory is not just someone making up an idea about something. So, if you hear the objection that "**evolution** is just a theory," the person making it has no understanding of what a **scientific theory** really is. **Gravity** is also a theory, by the way, and people don't expect that we'll go hurling into space if we stop "believing" it. In science, a theory is a set of explanations for a group of observable facts. Theories can (and should) be modified as new information is acquired, but for something to be labeled a scientific theory, it must have considerable evidence and be testable. A theory will also predict findings from further observations. If something is a theory, it has passed rigorous testing and is the best explanation currently available.

# An asteroid did not kill all the dinosaurs.

We know that, about sixty-six million years ago, a massive **asteroid** (or possibly a **comet**, according to some recent suggestions) slammed into the planet in what is now the **Yucatán Peninsula**. That event set off what is known as the **K–Pg Extinction** and ended the reign of the dinosaurs as the dominant animal species on Earth, paving the way for other animals, including us humans, to eventually emerge. But evidence has emerged that some species of dinosaurs may have lived on for as long as half a million years after the impact. And of course, not all of them died out; some survived and went on to evolve into our feathered friends, birds. So, while there are (thankfully!) no **T-Rexes** wandering about these days, every time a sparrow or a robin lands on your windowsill, you're technically looking at a dinosaur.

# Diamonds are not highly compressed coal.

A popular fallacy is that diamonds come from coal that has been compressed under extreme pressure. In fact, most diamonds formed before the first land plants even appeared; these plants are the main source of modern coal. So where do diamonds come from? Most diamonds that end up being sold commercially first formed in the mantle of the earth and were pushed upward by volcanic activity. So just putting some heavy weight on a lump of coal won't get you anything, other than smashed coal. Sorry!

# The earth's core is not molten lava.

Science fiction movies and scenes of hot, molten lava spewing out of the earth give us the impression that it must be all molten at its core, impossibly hot metals swirling in a fiery ocean that's so hot, it can never solidify. But in fact, the inner core of the earth is solid iron, surrounded by a molten outer core, which is itself surrounded by the magma layer (that's the lava!). This inner core was also liquid in the earth's younger days, but it has been slowly cooling down and solidifying and expanding ever since, though at an extremely slow rate. In fact, this slow cooling causes the outer molten core to swirl and churn, which gives us our protective magnetic field. At some point in the very far future, the core will cool completely, and the magnetic field will disappear. Earth will be more like Mars then.

# A particle accelerator will not kill us all.

There have been persistent rumors about the **Large Hadron Collider (LHC)** in Switzerland, which is used to smash particles together and study them. According to these doomsday purveyors, if those running the experiments are not careful, they could end up creating a mini black hole that could suck in the entire Earth, destroying everything. This fear was worked its way into the popular imagination and even jokes about the LHC causing different timelines, but the reality is, nothing of the sort is going to happen. Maybe there's a tiny chance that something could go wrong, but **Stephen Hawking** summed it up well, saying, "Collisions releasing greater energy occur millions of times a day in the earth's atmosphere and nothing terrible happens." So that's that, then.

# Mercury is not the hottest planet in the solar system.

**Mercury** is the closest planet to the sun in our solar system, and its surface is certainly hot. It can reach temperatures of 800°F on its daytime side, while plummeting to -290°F during Mercurian nights. But the hottest planet in the solar system is the next one out, **Venus**. This is because, unlike Mercury, Venus has an atmosphere, and a very thick one, composed almost entirely of **carbon dioxide**, or **CO2**. This is one of the classic **"greenhouse gases"** that is causing so much worry on our planet, as we keep pumping it into our own atmosphere. As a result of this CO2 atmosphere, heat from the sun gets in, but is trapped and can't radiate back out into space. Thus, Venus has an average temperature of 864°F, making it even hotter than the planet that is far closer to the sun.

# The sun will not explode or become a black hole at the end of its life.

You might hear these two possibilities tossed round from time to time. The fact is, the sun doesn't have enough energy to collapse into a **black hole**, or to explode. It would need much more energy and mass for either of those weird fates to happen. Instead, our relatively small star will begin to expand in size, like, way out. It will engulf **Mercury** and **Venus**, and possibly even Earth as it becomes, temporarily, a **red giant**. After that it will collapse into a **white dwarf**, the remains of a star that still glows from the leftover heat.

# Alcohol does not kill brain cells.

The subject of many health warnings, and many jokes, the truth is that alcohol does not, in and of itself, kill brain cells, at least not in a healthy adult. But, as everyone knows, what it does do is inhibit the communications between **dendrites**, the connecting endings of **neurons** that send and receive information. In other words, the drinker gets drunk. Someone who has been abusing alcohol excessively for years might suffer various kinds of brain damage, but that is a result of the effects of alcohol on the body over time (such as malnutrition), rather than the alcohol itself going to the brain and "killing" cells.

# Truth serum does not force you to tell the truth.

It's a great trope from spy movies and the like: inject someone with a **"truth serum,"** and they'll be forced to reveal the location of the secret hideout, no matter how much they try to resist. The reality is that "truth serums," which can be any number of different drugs, are most often nervous system depressants, or "downers," which essentially slow down one's thinking processes, and can make it more difficult to quickly think up a lie, but that's very different from them "forcing" someone to tell the truth (there are no drugs that can do that, thankfully). And there is no guarantee that the subject is not still lying; it varies from person to person. Given the ethical implications, truth serums are not only a waste of time, but also potentially dangerous, even if they are still occasionally used.

# Cars don't usually explode when the gas tank is hit by a bullet or anything else.

It makes for great action sequences in movies: the villain is trying to get away and the hero shoots the gas tank, making the car go boom. But in fact, modern automobiles are overengineered for safety, and gas tanks are not really susceptible to just exploding at the drop of a hat (or a bullet). Think about how cars get recalled if there is even one loose part in the airbag that could fly out and hit someone when it deploys. If exploding gas tanks were that common, the manufacturer would have to make a massive recall to fix the problem.

# Stars don't twinkle.

With apologies to the beloved children's song (which was *not* written by Mozart; see chapter 4), when you look at stars in the night sky, you're not seeing the light exactly as it is. The light from stars travels unimaginable distances through space before reaching Earth, but it still has to pass through the atmosphere before we see it. It's that process that bends and disturbs starlight, making it seem to flicker. It has nothing to do with the light itself, or the pulsing of the star the light came from. In fact, if you were to see the same light from the same star in space, there would be no twinkling at all.

# CHAPTER 3:
## Animals, Plants, and the Natural World

**The world around us is vast and mysterious,** and we're still exploring and learning about the natural world. While we've come a long way in our knowledge about the animals and plants we share this beautiful Earth with, there is much that remains unknown, and thousands of species that are still undiscovered. We all have bits of information that we've picked up over the years about animal and plant peculiarities, and while some of them are true, a surprising number are simply old tales that have long overstayed their welcome. Read on and be surprised about some things that you've been sure of for most of your life; you'll get a better understanding of the flora and fauna of the world.

# Frogs and toads do not cause warts.

It's like something out of a fairy tale. The young woman is afraid to kiss the frog because she might get a wart. It's thought that this belief came about because many frogs and toads have bumpy skin, which seems like it's covered in warts, but these are just a feature of their biology and have nothing to do with warts at all. Warts are caused by a virus that enters the skin through a cut or other entry point and sets up home there. Amphibians do not carry this virus and can't give you warts no matter how many you touch or how often you handle them.

# Bats are not blind.

While it's true that more than two-thirds of bats use **echolocation** (emitting high-pitched sounds and listening to the echo that returns) to find prey and navigate their surroundings, they have evolved to do this in the darkness of night, which is when they hunt. All bats have functioning eyes, and many species, such as fruit bats, have very good vision. **"Blind as a bat"** is not a thing!

# Elephants are not afraid of mice.

It's a cliché as old as cartoons and made famous by the movie *Dumbo*. The big, majestic elephant recoils in terror when the tiny little mouse goes scurrying by. It's funny, even charming, but there's not a bit of truth to it. It may date back to ancient Greece or Rome, where there were rumors that a mouse could crawl into an elephant's trunk and drive it crazy. But in fact, elephants are more startled by unexpected movements than by any particular creature. Experiments have proved this: holding up a mouse or two for an elephant to see gets no real reaction.

# Bulls do not get angry at the color red.

The image of the angry bull charging the matador is well known, and many assume that it must be the red-colored cape that they use that enrages the animal. But bulls actually can't see the color red at all. Like many animals, a bull has evolved to view only the colors it needs to see. Because it has limited color receptors in its eyes, the bull sees a cape more in a yellowish-gray color. It's the movements of the cape and the matador that get it wound up.

# Goldfish can remember things for much longer than a few seconds.

Goldfish are seen by many as cute and fairly dumb. It's long been believed that they can't remember anything for more than a few seconds. But this is simply not true. Experiments with feeding, such as putting food on a **Lego** block and then removing the block for a week or so, only to reintroduce it later, show that the goldfish can make associations and remember that food was on the block. Other studies have shown that goldfish can remember things for up to six months, if not longer. Goldfish can even recognize individual humans that feed them and remember them. It turns out that they are far smarter than they get credit for being!

# Duck quacks actually do echo.

This is a weird urban legend, but many still believe it. There are a few problems with it. First, there are several different kinds of quacks made by different ducks, so which one are we talking about? Second, most quacks have a sound with a diminishing volume at the end, making its echo harder to hear. Further, ducks tend to congregate in open areas, like lakes, where there is less of a chance that the sound will bounce off anything. But experiments with different species have definitely concluded that quacks of all kinds produce echoes in the right conditions.

# A mother bird will not reject its baby if it has been touched by a human.

You've probably heard this one: if you find a baby bird on the ground, don't touch it, because if it picks up a human scent, the mother will refuse to go near it. Most birds (with a few exceptions) don't have the greatest sense of smell to begin with. They are unlikely to be able to detect a "human scent" on their offspring, just because you picked one up and put it back in a nest. Many of the young birds you might see on the ground are **fledglings**, meaning that they have left the nest on their own and are capable of flying, at least short distances. If they have feathers, they are indeed fledglings, and it's probably fine to leave them alone. Their parents are likely nearby and watching them.

# Ostriches do not hide their heads in the ground.

Another classic misconception, found in many cartoons and artistic renderings, the idea is that ostriches are rather unintelligent and will hide their heads in the ground because they think that a predator won't be able to see them. And it's complete nonsense. Ostriches do bury their eggs in the ground and will often bend down to check on them. If they are in danger, they also might lower their heads to try to blend in with their surroundings, but this is far different from burying their heads, which would quickly make them suffocate!

# Birds will not die from eating wedding rice.

There is a belief that if birds ingest uncooked grains of rice, those grains will puff up in their stomachs, eventually rupturing their stomachs and killing them. There have even been some local laws based on this fear, making the throwing of wedding rice illegal. But while well intended, many birds not only eat rice, but also love the wild varieties. Their stomachs aren't going to inflate swallowed rice by that much, and experiments have shown that birdseed can inflate by even more. Other studies feeding birds a rice-only diet showed no discomfort at all, much less any deaths.

# One year for a dog does not always equal seven human years.

This model is sometimes used as a rule of thumb for how a dog ages, but it's not really accurate. A more accurate representation is that in the first year, a dog ages about fifteen human years, in the second year, they age about nine human years, and thereafter, it's about four or five human years per year. So a fifteen-year-old dog is in their late seventies to mid-eighties in human years, not over a hundred years by the seven years–per–year calculation.

# Lemmings do not commit mass suicide over cliffs.

This weird belief says that lemmings somehow know when they've overpopulated and will run in a pack to a cliff's edge, committing mass suicide to bring their population back down to safe levels. Lemming populations do bloom every few years, and sometimes they will travel as a group to find another area to live. They can swim and may cross water as a group to move to another area, so it's possible that a few might drown or die along the way, but there is no deliberate die-off. In fact, it's to try to preserve their numbers that they move at all.

# Sharks can get cancer.

The idea that sharks are immune to cancer is based on a misinterpretation of their biology. Some studies in the 1980s showed that their cartilage could prevent blood vessels from growing. Since cancer needs these to grow, it was assumed that sharks don't get cancer. Even worse, it started a market for people buying shark cartilage "supplements" to reduce their own cancer risks. But this is snake oil. Numerous studies have found examples of sharks with tumors and other cancers, even if their risk is somewhat reduced. And many sharks are endangered, so consuming their cartilage puts them at greater risk.

# There is no such thing as an "alpha" in a wolf pack.

This has been a thing with bros for a while. They like to go online and brag about being **"alpha males."** Or some of the more enterprising ones sell workshops and classes on how to become an "alpha." They base this on some wolf studies that were done in the 1970s, where wolves fought for dominance and to lead their packs. But here's the truth: these "alphas" were observed in captivity. In the wild, young wolves split off from their own packs and start new ones with a mate. The author of the original book has long since disavowed it. So, save your money on those "alpha male" workshops, guys.

# Snake jaws do not unhinge or dislocate.

Large snakes have been known to eat pigs, cattle, and even unfortunate humans. How can a snake possibly open its jaws wide enough to ingest something much bigger? They must dislocate their jaws to do it! Except they don't. This kind of snake's lower jawbone is not fused to the upper, but instead is held in place by ligaments that can stretch quite a bit. So, when the time comes to ingest a cow, or whatever, they can stretch those ligaments out to the size they need. It's still terrifying!

# Porcupines cannot launch their quills.

People are sometimes warned not to get too close to porcupines or to let their dogs get too close, because the animals can launch their very spiky quills in self-defense, and you could get shot with these natural darts. But in reality, that's not going to happen. These quills are used for self-defense and they do detach easily. This is helpful, because if a predator gets too close and brushes against said porcupine, it may end up running away with several painful quills stuck in it. But the porcupine is not able to shoot them on command like arrows, which is probably just as well.

# Mice do not love cheese more than other foods.

Ah, the mouse that gets the cheese! Such a happy creature! But there's no evidence that mice prefer cheese over other foods, despite the classic image of mousetraps using cheese as bait. Mice actually prefer crunchy things and sweets, and an experiment that put grapes and peanuts out with cheese showed that the mice loved the peanuts, and ate a grape or two, but left the little bits of cheddar untouched. Other studies have shown that mice really don't like cheese at all, and may be turned off by the aroma, even of milder cheeses. Another old wives' tale put to rest!

# Earthworms do not become two worms if cut in half.

Earthworms don't magically become two new creatures if you cut them in half, which is cruel anyway, so don't do it. They are capable of regrowing their tails if they lose those, but they have organs in their bodies, like other creatures, and if the head is severed or the portion of the body with the organs, called the saddle, is cut, they will die. There is a type of worm, the flatworm, that can do this little miracle, though. Cut off any part of it, and it will pretty much regrow a whole new worm. Not only that, but a flatworm can also regrow its head, and retain the memories it had before!

# Houseflies usually live for twenty to thirty days, not only twenty-four hours.

The idea that a housefly lives only for one day is pretty common, but if you've ever had one trapped in your home, you'll know that they can keep annoyingly buzzing around for days! A maggot will hatch about twenty-four hours after the egg is laid, so this may be where this misconception comes from. But once in fly form, the insect can buzz around for a much longer time. Some houseflies can live for as long as two months!

# The daddy longlegs spider is not the world's most venomous spider.

There are actually two different little creatures that can be called "daddy longlegs": **opilionids**, which have eight legs and are the "true" longlegs, and **pholcids**, which are actual spiders. Opilionids have no venom and eat mainly decaying vegetable matter, while pholcids are venomous, but almost never bite humans or bigger animals. Still, their venom has been tested and found to be mild and harmless to bigger creatures. So no, they are not the most venomous spiders in the world!

# Tomato juice does not remove the odor of a skunk's spray.

This is an old remedy for getting rid of the awful stink caused from a mishap with a skunk, but unfortunately, tomato juice does little or nothing to remove the smell. All it does is mask it for a little while, but once it wears off, sorry to say, the skunk odor comes right back. It's better to use hydrogen peroxide or baking soda when cleaning. Bleach is also effective, if the fabric can handle it. Don't waste your tomato juice; save it for the **Bloody Mary** you'll need after a run-in with a skunk!

# Evolution is not a progression from worse to better.

Saying that things evolve does not mean that they go only from simple to more complex or from "worse" to "better." The animals and plants alive today are not "better" than the ones that lived millions of years ago; they are simply the ones that have best adapted via natural selection to the changing environment. There are quite a few predators that were way better in the past (think of some dinosaurs!), but they had their time and then moved on, just as we will eventually. Organisms don't progress up the evolutionary tree so much as branch out.

# You should not suck the poison out of a snakebite.

This scenario has long been a favorite of westerns and survival films: a person is bit by a snake, and someone applies a tourniquet and sucks out the poison before it can spread. But, sorry to say, it doesn't work. The venom spreads too rapidly in the system, so all you'll be doing is risking infecting the wound. Also, while a tourniquet might stop the blood flow, it risks keeping the poison localized to that one area (an arm or leg, for example), which could cause permanent damage, or even result in the loss of the limb. The only real solution is to remain calm and seek medical attention as soon as possible.

# Elephants do not leave their herd and go to a "graveyard" when they are near death.

An old elephant knows when it's about to die and will break off from the herd and go to an **"elephant graveyard"** of others of their species to die in peace. Its pack may even visit its remains at some point. It's a touching story, but it's not true. Elephants do travel in herds and have migratory routes, but if an older elephant is weak, it will often stay in one place where there is food and protection, rather than risk traveling. If more than one does this, they might die in the same area, but the point is to try to survive, not to die.

# The ability of a bumblebee to fly is well understood.

You may have heard that a bumblebee, because of its size, shape, and wing placement, shouldn't actually be able to fly, and defies the laws of physics when it does. It's a great story, but it's not true. The idea probably started because some people assumed that bees fly like airplanes, which they don't. Their wings aren't stiff, and they rotate them to create tiny pockets of low air pressure to help them lift off. This has even been compared to creating tiny hurricanes! That's almost as cool as violating the laws of physics.

# Earwigs don't usually crawl into people's ears.

It's a thought that might make you squirm, and of course, these little insects must have gotten their name from the fact that they crawl into people's ears and lay their eggs, or eat their brains, right? Actually, no. Earwigs do live around houses and they have those little pincers that can hurt if they get you, but they have no interest in burrowing into your brain and setting up shop. Have a few earwigs crawled into unfortunate people's ears? Undoubtedly, but it's not a big risk. They prefer rotting wood, so unless you have that in your ears, you're probably pretty safe.

# Female praying mantises do not always eat males when mating.

Praying mantises are beautiful and strange insects that have an interesting (if bloody) legend about them: the female mates with the male and then bites of his head at its completion! It's the stuff of nightmares, but it's not true, at least not quite. There have been various studies that show that females eat parts of the male mate, about one-quarter of the time or less. There have also been studies that showed a male eating the female, and—get this—a male whose head was bitten off, but finished the job anyway! Also, these practices are more often observed in captivity, rather than in the wild.

# Sunflowers do not always point toward the sun.

Well, they got the name "sunflower" for a reason, right? The wonderful word **"heliotropism"** defines their movement in following the sun as it crosses the sky each day. But this tracking only happens in young flowers. Once they reach maturity, they will face forever eastward, watching the sun rise, but never seeing it set. It's rather sad and poetic. On the plus side, pollinators prefer east-facing blooms (they warm up faster), so sunflowers are guaranteed lots of visitors as they get older!

# Dogs do not sweat by salivating.

Dogs pant when they are hot, or nervous, or for other reasons, but that's not their equivalent of sweating. Dogs actually do sweat through glands in their paws. On hot days, their paws will get damp and they will leave wet paw prints. They don't have sweat glands on the rest of their bodies, because, like so many other mammals, they are covered in fur, and the sweat would not evaporate (the cooling mechanism). But their paws are bare skin, and sweating works the same for them there as it does for humans. So just remember, paws not pants!

# Cats and dogs are not color-blind.

It was long thought that most animals can only see in black and white, including cats and dogs. But like our eyes, theirs have what are called cone photoreceptors, which are cells that allow us to see various colors. Humans have three: red, blue, and green photoreceptors, which allow us the see the full palette of colors that we do. Cats and dogs, on the other hand, only have the blue and green receptors, so they don't perceive all the colors that we do. They can tell red from blue, but not red from green, for instance. Humans with color-blindness have similar limitations. And amazingly, there are animals that can see more colors than we can! We can't even imagine what those colors would look like!

# Elephant trunks are not straws.

Elephant trunks are unique, charming, and fun to watch. But one thing they are not is straws that suck up water into the elephant's body. They do use their trunks for a lot of things, though, including drinking. So, what are they doing? Well, their trunks are kind of like straws, but they are also noses. So, they "inhale" water only a short distance up the trunk and then pour it into their mouths. If they were to inhale water all the way up, they would choke just as we do if we get water up our noses or in our windpipes.

# Chameleons do not change their color to match their backgrounds.

Many people think that one of the chameleon's great talents is being able to change into any color and match its background to hide. But that's not why they change color; they do it in response to things like light, because of their mood, because of the outside temperature, and even to communicate. Many also have a limited number of colors that they can change to, maybe no more than three or four, while others might be able to change into several more. But this ability has little to do with hiding or matching their backgrounds.

# Milk isn't good for house cats.

The cat lapping at a saucer of milk or cream is a time-honored image, but the truth is, cow's milk really isn't good for them. Many cats are lactose intolerant, and milk (other than their mother's when they are kittens) doesn't provide enough nutrients. It can also cause gastrointestinal distress, diarrhea, vomiting, and a host of other complaints. So, don't give your cat milk, and don't pour it on their food. It will do them more harm than good!

# Mount Everest is not the world's tallest mountain.

This is a statement that needs a little qualification. **Mount Everest** stands at 29,029 feet, making it indeed the highest point on earth at mean sea level, but, strangely, another mountain, **Mount Chimborazo** in Ecuador, is slightly higher due to the bulge of the planet near its equator (the earth is not a perfect sphere); it's a mile farther away from the center of the earth than Everest. And we should also factor in **Mauna Kea**, the volcano on **Hawaii's Big Island**. From its base on the ocean floor to its peak, it rises an incredible 33,500 feet!

# Bears do not hibernate.

Another beloved belief: We think of bears as lumbering giants that store up on food as autumn sets in and then settle down for a long winter's nap, only to resurface in the spring. But bears not go into the state of hibernation for the entire winter. Rather, they enter a state called **torpor**. What's the difference? Well, both are deeply relaxed states, but in true hibernation, the animal will not wake up under any circumstances, while in torpor, sounds and other outside disturbances will cause them to wake up and be ready for dangers. Female bears can also wake up from torpor to give birth. But saying that bears enter torpor for the winter is probably not as fun as saying that they hibernate, so the misconception persists.

# You cannot charm a snake with music.

In fact, the snakes do not have external ears, and are virtually deaf. Instead, they feel vibrations and low-frequency sounds. So, the vibration of the **punji**, a reed instrument made from a gourd, draws the snake out, and then the swaying motion of the instrument captivates it. Its eyes are following the movement of the instrument, not the melody, and it's not "charmed." It's a defensive positon. A dangerous gig for the musician, to be sure!

# You cannot tell the age of a rattlesnake by counting its rattles.

Rattlesnakes are not like trees and tree rings. It used to be thought that they added one new rattle each year of their life, but it doesn't quite work that way. They gain a new rattle each time they shed their skin, but this can happen more than once a year. Typically, a snake will shed its skin once or twice a year, but under certain conditions, it may increase that to three or four times a year. So, just counting the number of segments on the rattle will not tell you how many years old the rattlesnake is.

# Cats purr for many reasons.

The sound of a cat purring is one that many find soothing and delightful. We like to think that a purring cat is a happy cat, and very often, that's true; they are content and turn the motor on. But cats can purr for other reasons, too. Cats also purr when they are frightened, or hungry, or distressed. One of the more intriguing things about purring is that the frequency (about 26 Hertz) helps with bone and tissue regeneration. So, an injured cat might purr to help itself heal. And not only house cats purr. Big cats like cheetahs and cougars can also get the motor running.

# Rattlesnakes do not always rattle before striking.

More rattlesnake facts! The rattle is a unique feature of these snakes and its distinct sound may be enough to frighten anyone away. And that's the whole point. The rattling is done as a warning. The snake may be warning the intruder to leave its space, or it may feel threatened. If it is cornered, the rattling may be a sign that it is about to strike, but a snake that is hunting will not rattle (scaring off its prey), and the rattling does not mean the snake will bite. If you encounter a rattling snake, back away slowly; it's warning you to get away from it, and if you do, it won't strike.

# Piranhas cannot devour someone in seconds.

These strange, toothy fish have been the villains in many a horror film, and the idea of them being able to reduce a bigger animal or human to bone in a minute or two is terrifying. But these small fish tend to avoid much larger creatures in the water, unless they are in a very large school. President Teddy Roosevelt once said that he saw a school of piranhas devour a cow in minutes, but modern biologists have said this would have had to been a very large school and a very small cow. It would take literally up to five hundred of them to devour a human in five minutes. But most of the time, they are quite happy just munching on smaller fish and even plants.

# You can teach an old dog new tricks.

It's a saying way older than the old dog, but the funny thing is, you can teach an old dog new tricks. In fact, older dogs can be easier to train than puppies, who have boundless energy and get easily distracted. Older dogs are a bit more mellow and can stay focused on the task longer. Dogs are inherently curious animals and can learn new things throughout their lives. So go ahead and teach your older dog something new!

# Boa constrictors do not suffocate their prey.

You would think that a giant snake like a boa constrictor would easily be able to suffocate whatever it wrapped itself around. But that's not how they actually kill their prey. What they actually do is constrict (hence the name) the flow of blood to the prey's vital organs. This lack of blood quickly causes organs to shut down; starved of oxygen, they begin to die. The blood pressure drops, and the heart is affected, and soon, the snake has a tasty meal. But suffocating them had nothing to do with it.

# Camels do not store water in their humps.

These "ships of the desert" are known for being able to live and even thrive in very hot and dry places. Their famed humps were thought by many to be storage tanks for water, to let them go for long periods of time without drinking. But actually, those humps store fat, fat that can be used as nutrients when food is scarce. As they use it up, the humps will begin to sag, but once they've eaten enough, they'll pop right back up. As for water, a camel can drink twenty to thirty gallons (!) of water in one go, and it stores that water in its bloodstream. A camel can go for a week or more without drinking water.

# Wolves are not usually aggressive.

Despite the image of snarling, hungry wolves, waiting in the forests to devour the unwary (think **"Little Red Riding Hood"**), wolves are not generally that aggressive. A slight increase in wolf attacks in recent decades has more to do with people encroaching more into natural areas that were once wolf habitats and the wolves returning than it does with any aggression. Wolves will snarl and howl at intruders, but usually will not attack unless they feel threatened or are starving or have rabies or some other ailment. In general, they are shy creatures who try to avoid humans as much as possible, and who can blame them?

# Owls cannot spin their heads 360 degrees.

No, owl heads aren't just resting up there and spinning any way they want them to, but they are remarkable twisty. While they can't do a full 360-degree turn, they can spin their heads around a remarkable 270 degrees! This means that they can turn their head all the way around behind them, a very useful trait when hunting for prey. They can do this in part because the blood vessels in and around their necks tend to relax as they turn (in most animals they constrict), thus not interfering with blood flow. So, while they don't spin their heads all the way round, they can do the next best thing!

# Turkeys actually can fly.

We tend to see turkeys wandering along on the ground, their plumage folded up, parading around like the little dinosaurs that they are. Only occasionally will they go full **Thanksgiving** and spread their feathers out. But many people assume that turkeys can't fly, when, in fact, they can. They roost in trees for the night, so they have to be able to get up there somehow! Also, they can reach speeds of up to 55 mph for short periods of time, such as when they need to get away from danger. And they can swim!

# Not all cats hate water.

It's a cliché that's only partly true. Some cats do hate water, other than drinking it, preparing to wash themselves with their tongues, as nature intended. But some cats, like the **Turkish Van** breed, actually love water and can swim quite well. House cats are descended from the little desert cats of the Middle East, most of whom lived in very dry climates. So, they're not biologically "wired" for large amounts of water and may be afraid of it. But some bigger cats, like tigers, love water and will go for swims regularly.

# Wolves do not howl at the moon.

Blame it on the werewolf, or maybe images of lonely wolves in the middle of the forest at night, heads raised and howling at the moon. It's a striking image, but it is true? In a word, no. Numerous studies have been conducted that found no connection between howling and the presence of the moon, full or otherwise. Wolves tend to be more nocturnal, which is probably where the association comes from. But they howl to assemble their pack, to let other wolves in the pack know where they are, and sometimes as a warning to other wolves not in the pack to stay away. It's also a way of bonding and maybe even a means of stress relief. If the moon happens to be overhead, well, that's just a coincidence.

# Giraffes sleep for more than thirty minutes a day.

Giraffes are wonderfully strange and seemingly improbable creatures that have many interesting facts attached to them, such as having blue-purple tongues. But one thing you might have heard about them—that they only sleep for thirty minutes a night—isn't true, at least not quite. It is true they don't need a lot of sleep and might only sleep for up to four hours a day. They might do some of that in separate sleeps and naps, but it's still considerably more than only a half hour a day. Still, compared to a lion that might sleep twenty or more hours a day, it's not a lot, and probably developed as a defense against predators, like said lions. An awake giraffe can run at up to 35 mph, after all.

# Most bees can sting more than once.

Bad news for people with bee phobias: wasps and most bees can sting more than once. It's really only the honeybee that suffers this fate. That's because the honeybee has a hook in its stinger that holds the stinger under the skin of the animal or human it has stung. When it tries to fly away, the stinger will rip out of its body, killing the bee. Other stinging insects, like bumblebees and carpenter bees, don't have this feature, though, so they can sting again and again. The good news is that bees aren't usually aggressive if you leave them alone. They don't fly around looking for things to sting, so don't give them a reason to!

# Plants release both oxygen and carbon dioxide.

It's a common misconception that plants "breathe in" carbon dioxide, and "breathe out" oxygen, replenishing our atmosphere's supply. While this isn't entirely untrue, plants actually release both, depending on whether or not they are engaging in photosynthesis. During the daylight hours, when a plant is exposed to sunlight, it will absorb carbon dioxide and release oxygen, but at night, it will do the opposite.

# CHAPTER 4:
# Culture and Lifestyles

**"Culture" includes so many concepts and ideas** that there's no way to define it or do justice to it in a short little introduction like this. Consider this final chapter to be something of a miscellany of topics of all sorts: beliefs, music, movies, sports, society, fads, food and drink, and more. Everything around us is subject to misunderstanding, and with the arrival of the internet, these misconceptions not only flourish, but also will become much worse and more widespread in the coming decades. Just think about how much nonsense you see online in any given week, or even day! The entries in this section will allow you to be armed against some of the more commonly held erroneous beliefs out there.

# The Inuit and Aleut do not have significantly more words for snow.

There have been many claims about this: the **Inuit** and **Aleut**, the northern native peoples of Alaska and Canada, have a large number of words for "snow." It varies between fifty and even four hundred, but it's not true, at least not in the way that people think of it. The misconception seems to have started with an anthropologist named **Franz Boas** in 1911 and was popularized by others later on. The truth is that there are many different languages among these peoples, so yes, there will be many different words for snow, and they will have different terms, just as English does for "snow," "sleet," "snowbank," "frost," etc. But that doesn't mean there are hundreds of different words for snow in one language.

# The Chevrolet Nova actually sold well in Latin American countries.

It's a long-standing joke that when **General Motors** introduced its **Chevrolet Nova** model to various Latin American countries, it failed to sell, because the word "nova" translates into Spanish as "doesn't go." And who would want to buy a car with a name like that? But this never happened. The Nova sold well enough in Venezuela and Mexico. "Nova" is one word, while "no go" would literally be *no va*. Despite the humor about the perils of failing to do market research, there is no evidence that the company had any issues with sales at all.

# The Bible does not record that there were three wise men.

The image of the wise men visiting the infant Jesus is known throughout the world, especially in nativity scenes and other **Christmas** imagery. Almost always, these scenes show three wise men, bringing their gifts of gold, frankincense, and myrrh. So, by tradition and association, it's been assumed that there was one wise man per gift, which makes sense. But the **Bible** only says that wise men came from the East; it makes no mention of the number. The names **Gaspar**, **Melchior**, and **Balthasar** only appear several centuries later. Indeed, in some Eastern Christian traditions, such as the **Syriac Church**, there are twelve wise men; that would make the nativity scene a little crowded!

# The word "jihad" does not only mean "holy war."

It's become a buzzword for terrorism over the last several decades, as militant Muslim groups like to proclaim that they are launching a **jihad** against a group, a country, etc. It's also a term that has been widely misunderstood outside of the Islamic world, with everyone from politicians to journalists misusing it for their own purposes. But the word "jihad" actually translates to "struggle," and means, first, the inner struggle to become a better Muslim; second, the struggle to build a good and just society; and third, a defensive struggle against outside attack. There are certainly groups that use the word as an excuse to launch terrorist attacks and other aggression, but that's not the original intent of the word.

# A fatwa is not an Islamic death sentence.

A **fatwa** is simply a nonbinding opinion on a certain religious issue or matter by an Islamic scholar or court. The confusion came after British/Indian author **Salman Rushdie** wrote his 1988 book, ***The Satanic Verses***, which caused anger and outrage in some Muslim countries, especially Iran and Pakistan. Iran's leader, **Ayatollah Ruhollah Khomeini**, issued a ruling that permitted Muslims to kill Rushdie and his publishers, or at least help those who could. There was a strong backlash against this ruling, with many defending Rushdie on the grounds of free speech. Rushdie went into hiding and the fatwa remains in place, since it can only be rescinded by the one who issued it, and Khomeini died in 1989. In any case, a fatwa can be issued about any topic and does not have the force of law.

# The term "420" did not come from the Los Angeles police or a penal code for marijuana.

A popular term with pot smokers that many have thought came either from a police code for marijuana possession, or from a California penal code describing its use as unlawful. But neither of these explanations is true. There is a **California Senate Bill 420**, but that refers to medical marijuana and was named for the number, not the other way around. The term seems to date from 1971, when students at San Rafael High School in Northern California would agree to meet at a statue of **Louis Pasteur** at 4:20 in the afternoon to smoke. **"420 Louis"** was their code phrase. Fans of **The Grateful Dead** picked up on the phrase, and it circulated into wider use.

# The word "Xmas" was not an attempt to "remove Christ from Christmas."

Some have claimed that the abbreviation *Xmas* is a way of dechristianizing **Christmas**, to make the holiday more secular, when in fact nothing could be further from the truth. The abbreviation dates back to the early Middle Ages, and the Greek letter χ pronounced "chi," with the *ch* as in the Scottish word *loch*. **Christ**, or "Christos" in Greek, was thus written as *Χριστος*. The *X* came to be used as shorthand in Latin writings as well, where they might write *Xstos*, for example. So, when writing the word "Christmas," monks and other scholars would sometimes abbreviate it to "Xmas." The abbreviation actually came from Christians who wanted to save time in writing it out!

# Coca-Cola did not invent the popular image of Santa Claus.

There's a popular urban legend that goes around from time to time saying that our modern version of **Santa Claus** was actually a creation of the **Coca-Cola Company** in the 1930s to help sell their drink. The red and white, so the legend goes, are actually the colors of the coke bottle or can. While it's true that the company made use of him in their advertising (and quite successfully), the red and white Santa and other versions of **Father Christmas** had already been around for a lot longer. Our modern Santa is a hybrid of several traditions, and no one person or organization created him.

# Orson Welles's radio broadcast of H. G. Wells's *War of the Worlds* did not cause widespread panic.

It's a great story: **Orson Welles** did a radio broadcast of the famous science fiction story ***The War of the Worlds*** on October 30, 1938. Listeners thought it was a real news broadcast and began to panic, especially in the New York and New Jersey areas, calling their local police and government, asking what to do. Newspapers even reported on the mass hysteria that the broadcast caused, saying that countless people fled their homes to go and hide. But recent studies have shown that reports of this mass panic were almost all anecdotal and picked up by news outlets because they sounded like good stories. The story was cemented by a sociology study written two years afterward that used the press reports of the incident as proof. But if some people genuinely freaked out about the broadcast, it was a small number.

# The deep web is not the dark web.

These two webs are often confused with each other. The **dark web** has taken on a sinister reputation as a place where all manner of illegal activity and depravity happens, everything from drug and prostitution sales to full-on live-cam murder rooms. The **deep web** has become associated with this same activity. But the deep web simply means the part of the web that is not accessible to regular searches. It's where passwords and personal information are stored: for example, financial records and some kinds of classified information. In fact, the deep web makes up most of the internet by far. The surface web, what we can access through searches and visits, accounts for way less than 1 percent of the total internet! And the dark web is even less than that.

# The United States spends far less on foreign aid than people think.

It's a common complaint that can cross the political divide: The United States spends far too much on foreign aid and should spend that money at home instead. It's a great talking point, especially during elections, but there's no real truth to it. Some make the wild claim that foreign aid is almost one-third of the total US budget, which is completely absurd. Even if more realistic numbers are used, say one-tenth, it's still way off. The actual amount? Less than 1 percent. And it pays off in other ways. Of the United States' fifteen biggest trading partners today, eleven used to be recipients of our aid. So, take any arguments against this aid based on numbers with a large grain of salt.

# You do not need to wait thirty to sixty minutes after eating before you swim.

Many people who love getting out in summer weather have heard that they had to be careful about swimming too soon after lunch, or breakfast, or whatever. The thought was that since some of our blood is needed in the digestion process, it's not wise to move too soon after a meal. It seems to make sense, but as far as swimming goes? There's no real evidence that swimming soon does any harm. So, you can set aside those fanciful urban legends about people getting severe muscle or stomach cramps and drowning because they only waited ten minutes after eating. Unless you're about to go into an Olympic competition, you'll probably be fine.

# Sugar does not make children hyper.

Sugar is fuel, so it makes sense that if a child overloads on it, they will be a little energy machine, and start running around like crazy, right? Except that hyperactivity has nothing to do with sugar intake. This connection was based on a single study in the 1970s that has since been debunked dozens of times. While it's true that eating too much sugar in general is bad for everyone, kids have a lot of energy, and sometimes it just comes out.

# Chewing gum does not take seven years to digest if you swallow it.

This weird urban legend has been told and retold by countless children, sometimes with gruesome details about what would happen if they accidentally swallowed their gum. The bigger misconception is that gum is not digestible and will sit in your stomach for seven years while it's slowly broken down. While it's true that gum isn't really digested, the good news is that, like everything else in your stomach, it will pass on into the intestines to be pooped out later. If one were to swallow a large amount of gum, it might cause some constipation, but you can safely ignore the horror stories and not worry if it actually slips down your gullet once in a while.

# Fortune cookies were not invented in China.

Though we see them in nearly every Chinese restaurant in the United States and beyond, they aren't Chinese. There are a few competing stories about where they come from: something resembling a fortune cookie was found in Japan in the nineteenth century, and the **Japanese Tea Garden** in San Francisco claimed to have first served them around 1890. The **Hong Kong Noodle Company** in Los Angeles also claimed to have invented these cookies, around 1918, but a court ruled in favor of the Tea Garden's claim. The **Fugetsu-Do confectionary shop** in Los Angeles also took credit for inventing them, so the matter is not settled. In any case, they don't come from China, and attempts to make them popular there in recent years have mostly failed!

# Bananas do not grow on trees.

Bananas grow on very large plants that look like trees. These plants can reach thirty feet in height or more, and they are very sturdy, but the stems contain no wood tissue or bark; they are instead very dense packs of leaves. The banana "tree" is technically a perennial herb. Also, bonus fact: bananas are actually berries.

# Twinkies are not edible for decades.

It's a popular and even funny bit of junk food lore: **Twinkies** are basically immortal. They're not made with any "real" food ingredients, and so they never spoil. They'll survive a nuclear war, or well into the next Ice Age, and you don't even have to do anything. If there's one thing you want in your survival bunker, it's a generous helping of Twinkies! But the reality is that Twinkies are baked like every other cake item, and do contain eggs, sugar, flour, and oil, among other ingredients. Here's the big shocker: their shelf life is only about twenty-five days. So, if you're stocking up on them for the apocalypse, you might be very disappointed.

# Seeds are not the spiciest part of a chili pepper.

A lot of recipes will tell you to remove the seeds from a chili if you want to bring down the spiciness, but they're just having you on. There is heat on the seeds, but it's not where the main concentration of a chili's spice is. The heat comes from a chemical compound called **capsaicin**, and it is much more concentrated in the pith, the white lining inside. The seeds that come into contact with this lining will pick up some of the heat, but the spiciness is not in the seeds themselves. So, remove this white lining if you want to cool down your chili a little, and make sure to wash your hands!

# Turkey meat does not make you sleepy.

You know the feeling after a big **Thanksgiving** meal: you loosen your belt, you flop on the couch, and then the post-meal drowsiness sets in. It's all that **tryptophan** in the turkey, right? Actually, no. Tryptophan is an essential amino acid, and one that promotes sleep, and turkey definitely has some in it, but not nearly enough to make you pass out after a meal. You'd need to eat something like twenty slices of turkey to feel the effects! And maybe you did; in which case, you can skip on to the next entry. But for most people, turkey alone isn't enough to induce drowsiness. If you've had the full Thanksgiving holiday meal with potatoes, stuffing, pies, etc., you'll likely have a spike in blood sugar, which can make you feel sleepy. Throw in some wine with that, and you'll be out cold on the couch before too long!

# Tomatoes do not ripen best in the sun.

It seems obvious that tomatoes, which thrive in hot, sunny climates, are sun-loving fruits that turn a deep red the longer they sit out in the sun. But they really ripen in heat, and they ripen better when it's not too hot. Temperatures in the mid-seventies Fahrenheit are ideal for producing great tomatoes. Tomatoes that are outside and ripening in hotter temperatures can actually suffer what is called "sunscald," being burned by the sun, which can inhibit proper ripening. And of course, colder temperatures do them no good, either. It's the sun's heat, not its light, that does the ripening job.

# Henry Ford did not invent the automobile.

**Henry Ford** is probably more associated with the automobile than any other person in history. His **Ford Motor Company** was one of the key providers of cars in the early days of America's growing infatuation with private transport, beginning in 1903. But Ford didn't invent the car. Most historians now credit the German inventor **Karl Benz** with that honor, though there were several other inventors working on the idea of a self-propelling transport machine at the time. Benz created a three-wheeled vehicle in 1885 that ran on gasoline, and he exhibited his work at the **Paris World's Fair** in 1889. Ford completed his first automobile in 1896.

# Microwave ovens do not cook food from the inside out.

This is a common misconception about how a **microwave** works. They actually heat from the outside in, just like other heating methods. Microwaves emit short radio waves that bounce around inside the cooking area of the oven. When they strike fats, sugars, and other substances, they heat them up very quickly. But in order to heat the inside up, they still have to pass through the outside first. Of course, this heating doesn't always occur evenly, which is one of the reasons for the spinning tray in many microwaves. So, some parts may be hotter than others, but that doesn't mean the inside is being heated up first.

# Microwave ovens do not cause cancer.

It's another **microwave** misconception, but these handy little machines don't cause cancer. The waves used to heat the food, as mentioned, are high-frequency radio waves, but these waves are not at a harmful frequency and do not make your food radioactive. Also, when the machine is turned off, there aren't any lingering radioactive waves inside the cooking chamber when you reach in to take out your food. The only real risk you might have with a microwave is burning yourself on very hot food, so be careful when taking it out!

# There is little to no evidence that "detox" diets work.

**Detox** and cleansing diets and drinks have been a big thing for a long time, but do they really do anything at all? The answer is: they don't do much. You have a liver and kidneys that, if working properly, should do all the detoxifying you need. There is evidence that fasting under medical supervision can bring some genuine health benefits, but special cleansing diets? Not so much. People might feel good doing them simply because they're eliminating unhealthy foods for the duration, but that's more to do with what people are putting into their bodies, rather than cleansing anything out.

# Alcohol does not warm the body.

This is a common and dangerous misconception. If you've ever had a strong drink, it might burn the back of your throat, so it stands to reason that alcohol must be warming in some way. But the truth is, alcohol actually cools the body, even if it makes you feel warm. Alcohol dilates blood vessels and inhibits your ability to shiver, which is a natural reaction that does warm you up. Alcohol will also make you sweat, which just cools you down even further. So, the old image of the St. Bernard dog bringing the stranded person in the Alps some strong drink to warm them is not only false, but also if consumed in those conditions, it could be dangerous.

# Spicy food does not cause ulcers.

Some people love spicy foods, some hate them, but some believe that ingesting too many chilies and peppers can actually cause damage to the body, especially the stomach. Can too many chilies give you ulcers? No, ulcers are usually caused by the bacterium *Helicobacter pylori*, which burrows into the stomach lining and grows. Antibiotics are the normal treatment. Interestingly, **capsaicin**, the chemical that gives chilies their heat, has been shown in various studies to help inhibit acid production in the stomach, so they definitely don't cause ulcers, though the heat can sometimes make them feel worse.

# Brown sugar is not really any healthier than white sugar.

Possibly inspired by the brown rice/white rice comparison, or even whole wheat bread and white bread, many people think that brown sugar is somehow healthier than more refined white sugar. Brown sugar is produced either by processing it less so that it retains some of its brown color and molasses, or it's just white sugar to which some molasses has been added back in (yes, really!). Both have almost the same number of calories, and while brown sugar has trace amounts of nutrients, none of these are present in any significant amount. Sorry to say, but sugar is sugar.

# Breakfast is not the most important meal of the day.

You've probably heard this one many times. You need to fuel up early, or otherwise you'll be failing by lunchtime and won't catch up. There have been several studies that have shown that eating breakfast can be good for weight loss and weight control, but guess who commissioned those studies? That's right, breakfast cereal companies! That doesn't automatically invalidate them, of course, but it might make you a little suspicious. Another study showed that those who didn't eat breakfast gained only about one pound over the duration of the study, and this could easily be because they were eating a bit more at lunch. There is in fact, evidence that intermittent fasting (eating only between eight or nine hours a day) can be very good for weight control, and many who do this skip breakfast altogether.

# The order you drink alcohol in has little effect on intoxication or side effects.

You may have heard the old saying: "Beer before liquor, never been sicker; liquor before beer, you're in the clear." But does the order in which you consume alcoholic drinks have anything to do with how drunk you get, or the kind of hangover you'll risk? Not really. It might be that drinking spirits, which are higher in alcohol, makes one not drink as much or as quickly, while beer, which is lower in alcohol, may encourage someone—once they're a bit drunk—to move on to the hard stuff afterward. In which case, yes, the saying could be true. But it's nothing to do with the type of alcohol; rather, it's the amount and the speed at which it is consumed.

# George Washington Carver did not invent peanut butter.

**George Washington Carver** was an amazing inventor who did indeed work with peanuts, finding ways to use them in sauces, shampoos, and even glue. But the one thing he didn't invent, despite stories to the contrary, is peanut butter. There is evidence that the **Aztec** and **Inca** peoples ground peanuts into paste long before anyone from Europe arrived. In Carver's own time (the later nineteenth century), others were already working on the idea. Canadian inventor **Marcellus Gilmore Edson** patented a peanut paste in 1884, while **Dr. John Harvey Kellogg** (of the cereal company) patented a way of making peanut butter from raw peanuts in 1895. Carver was hugely important in popularizing the peanut, but peanut butter was not one of his creations.

# Toilet waste is never deliberately flushed out of a commercial aircraft.

It's pretty horrifying and revolting idea: commercial airlines flying overhead simply flush their toilet contents out every time you push the handle. Other stories claim that waste is first frozen and then expelled in frozen chunks. Either way, it's an awful thought! But the truth is that airlines never do this on purpose. Waste is routed to a tank at the back of the plane (emptied after landing), and its extra weight is already calculated into what the plane can bear. Occasionally one of these tanks leaks and some waste may escape to be frozen and fall in someone's yard as poop ice, (ew!), but it's never on purpose!

# There was no dead Munchkin in a scene from *The Wizard of Oz.*

There's a macabre urban legend that an actor playing a **Munchkin** in the *Wizard of Oz* committed suicide by hanging himself from one of the fake trees, and that this wasn't known while filming, but can be seen in one instance where **Dorothy** and friends are skipping along the **Yellow Brick Road**. The real story is that the filmmakers borrowed some birds from a local zoo to bring onto the set and give the woods a more "real" feeling. There is indeed a large bird in the background, probably a crane, and people mistook it for a suicidal Munchkin. The truth is almost as strange, but there you have it!

# Mozart did not write "Twinkle, Twinkle, Little Star" when he was five years old.

**Mozart** was undoubtedly a musical genius who was writing complex pieces of music from an astonishingly young age, including a symphony at the age of eight! He is also credited with writing the music to the popular tune **"Twinkle, Twinkle, Little Star,"** which doesn't seem far-fetched for a young, budding musical genius to come up with. It's a simple little melody that could have been composed by him, but it wasn't. He did write variations on the tune in the 1780s, probably intended as practice pieces for his students, but the song already existed, and may date back to several decades before he was born. The English lyrics, by the way, weren't attached to the tune until 1838, long after Mozart had died.

# Musicians didn't hide backward satanic messages in records.

Back in the glory days of LP records (1960s–80s), a bizarre accusation was made against various rock bands, including **Led Zeppelin** and others. Certain anti-rock moral crusaders began accusing bands of hiding secret messages on their albums that could only be heard when they were played backward. These messages were, of course, praises to Satan and other diabolical entities, or invitations to drug use and other sins. It was, of course, the overactive imaginations of the zealous, because how would anyone hear these **"backmasked"** messages, anyway? However, many bands in response started having fun with this and began including backward messages, usually with joke messages in them. Be careful what you wish for!

# Walt Disney is not cryogenically frozen under Disneyland.

This odd urban legend has circulated widely. It's said that **Walt Disney's** body is cryogenically frozen and held in an underground vault, usually somewhere below the **"Pirates of the Caribbean"** ride. One day, when the science allows for it, he'll be revived. It's complete nonsense. The rumors started sometime after his death in 1966 and were amplified by two spurious and badly presented "biographies" of Walt that appeared in the 1980s and 1990s. His own family has denied that he had any interest in, or even knowledge of, cryonics, and public records show that he was cremated.

# Mozart was not poisoned by Salieri.

Thanks to the play and the movie *Amadeus*, a good number of people now know the story of **Salieri**, the mediocre composer who was jealous of **Mozart**, and worked behind the scenes to hinder his career. Ultimately, driven by that rivalry, he succeeded in murdering Mozart, or at least driving him to his death. And it's not true. Stories about Salieri disliking Mozart circulated in the early nineteenth century and were made popular in a play by the Russian writer **Alexander Pushkin**. It's possible that Mozart's own father encouraged some of these stories going back to the 1780s, since he seemed to think that Salieri was getting in Mozart's way. But Salieri revived some of Mozart's works, and the two even composed a cantata together. There's no reason to believe that he hated Mozart, and he was a far better composer than he was made out to be in the film and play.

# The MGM lion did not kill anyone.

Another popular entertainment urban legend is that the famed **MGM lion**, whose roar is seen in front of so many films, killed his trainer and two of the trainer's assistants the day after being filmed making the world-famous roar. In fact, there were several male lions used in those days of classic cinema, including lions named Leo (who has been appearing at the beginning of MGM films since 1957), Slats, and Jackie, and absolutely no record of them killing anyone, ever. This urban legend may have originated (or at least been amplified) by a satirical "fake news" website many years ago.

# Captain Kirk never said, "Beam me up, Scotty!"

At least not in that way. It's one of the clichés of **Star Trek** lore and has found its way into everyday conversation. But similar to **Sherlock Holmes's** oft misquoted "Elementary, my dear Watson," **Captain Kirk** didn't say those exact words. The closest he got was when he said, "Scotty, beam us up" in the episode "The Gamesters of Triskelion" and in a few other episodes. OK, that may be splitting hairs, but it's still different from the way most people remember the quote.

# The X rating was not created for porn films.

When the **Motion Picture Association (MPA)** created a rating system for films in 1968, it was a voluntary set of rules to give viewers and especially parents a guide to the content that a movie had, to make more informed viewing choices. Initially films could be classified as G, PG, R, and X. Genuine masterpieces such as *Midnight Cowboy* (1969) and *A Clockwork Orange* (1971) were X-rated films. But there was a problem; the MPA never trademarked the X rating, so beginning in the 1970s, porn films began using the designation as a badge of honor; *X* sounds like "sex," and it made their films seem more enticing by being forbidden in some way. The MPA created the PG-13 rating in the 1980s, and eventually responded with a new "official" adults-only rating, NC-17, in 1990, but this rating has mostly failed to work as intended, with many theaters refusing to show NC-17 films, insisting they be edited down to an R rating.

# Getting banned from a website doesn't violate your First Amendment rights.

This argument seems to have been used a lot in recent years. Someone says something outrageous online and the site suspends them or bans then, so they go elsewhere and complain about how they're being "censored." They have a **First Amendment** right to say what they want, after all, right? Well, no. The First Amendment only stipulates what the government can and cannot do. If the site is not government-run, then it's a private business or site. Social media sites can set their terms of use, something everyone agrees to when they check that box during sign-up, the one at the end of the long terms window that no one ever reads. Think of it as a digital version of "no shirt, no shoes, no service." If you don't abide by their terms, you can get the boot. It's really as simple as that.

# Abner Doubleday did not invent baseball.

It's a popular romanticized version of the origins of America's pastime. **Abner Doubleday** created the rules for **baseball** in 1839, when he lived in Cooperstown, New York. But Doubleday was not in Cooperstown in that year, and versions of baseball already existed, including **cricket** and **rounders**. Stickball games can be traced back as far as ancient Egypt and were popular in England going back to the Middle Ages. While they didn't have the exact same rules, the rules for modern baseball were created and adapted over a much longer period than one magical summer in 1839.

# Sex before a sporting event does not decrease performance.

It's a policy that even some modern sports coaches impose on their male players: no sex before a major event. The belief that sex can decrease athletic abilities probably goes back to ancient Greek times, and while some athletes swear by it, the limited amount of study that's been done on the subject has shown no clear connection. Some athletes say that the agitation and frustration caused by abstinence makes them sharper and hungrier for the victory. This might be true, and certainly getting enough sleep before an event is important, but there's no proven physical link between not getting any and better sports performance.

# Gold medals aren't made of gold.

At least not very much. Let's face it, gold is expensive, and to produce enough to make solid gold medals for an event such as the **Olympics** would probably be cost-prohibitive. Plus, they'd be really heavy! The gold medal, therefore, is mostly silver, with a thin coating of gold over the top. For the winner, it's not really the make-up of the medal that matters, anyway; it's the honor and the reward of the "gold" medal, regardless of its metallic content.

# The 1980 Winter Olympics "Miracle on Ice" was not the gold medal game.

It was a stunning upset that shocked the world. At the 1980 **Winter Olympics**, the **United States hockey team** pulled off a stunning victory over the heavily favored team from the Soviet Union. Many people think that this victory won them the gold medal, but it wasn't the game for the gold medal. The US team still had to face Finland in the final for a shot at winning the gold. And guess what? They won that match, too!

# Michael Phelps never ate 12,000 calories a day when training.

**Michael Phelps** is an Olympic swimming legend, the most decorated of all time, with twenty-eight medals to his name. So, it's only natural that people would wonder about his training regimen. For a while, a story circulated that, when preparing, he would consume 12,000 calories a day, since he would burn it all off during his rigorous training sessions. But Phelps himself shut down this rumor, even though it persists. Still, he confirmed that he did consume between 8,000 and 10,000 calories a day!

# Vince Lombardi didn't invent the saying: "Winning Isn't Everything, It's the Only Thing."

**Vince Lombardi**, the legendary coach of the **Green Bay Packers**, is often given credit for this quote, and it seems appropriate, given his career of winning teams and **Super Bowl** victories. But the quote seems to have originated with player and fellow coach **Red Sanders** (at **UCLA**), who used it in the early 1950s. Lombardi borrowed it for his speech in 1959 at the opening of the Green Bay Packers' training camp, but he definitely didn't invent it.

# Sherlock Holmes never said, "Elementary, my dear Watson."

**Sherlock Holmes** remains one of the most beloved fictional characters of the last century and more. And the "elementary" quote is by far the most famous saying attributed to him. But he never said it in any of **Arthur Conan Doyle's** original stories. He certainly used the words "dear Watson" on any number of occasions and did say "elementary" in *The Adventure of the Crooked Man* from 1893, but he never said the more famous phrase together until later, when both fans and then movie scripts put the words into his mouth.

# Marilyn Monroe never said, "Well-behaved women rarely make history."

Another famous misattributed quote, this one has been given to not only **Marilyn Monroe**, but also **Gloria Steinem** and **Eleanor Roosevelt**, among others. But it actually originated with **Laurel Thatcher Ulrich**, a professor at **Harvard University**. In 1976, she wrote a journal article about women in early America, and said, "Well-behaved women seldom make history," in discussing that those who went along with the laws and customs of the time were basically forgotten. Not long after, the word "seldom" was changed to "rarely," and the misattributions started.

# Phil Collins's hit song "In the Air Tonight" was not about him witnessing a drowning victim and then confronting the person who let it happen during a concert.

This is one of the more persistent pop music legends that still gets knocked about. Supposedly, as a boy, **Phil Collins** saw his friend drowning, but was too far away to help him, while a man who could have helped him stood by and did nothing. Collins later found out who it was, gave him a front-row ticket, and then sang the song, while a spotlight shone on the man. In some versions, the man later kills himself in shame. And it's all ridiculous. According to Collins himself, the song is actually about his bitterness over the end of his first marriage and doesn't reference any specific events at all.

# The black belt in martial arts does not represent an expert or master.

For many, the words **"black belt"** imply someone who has mastered a martial art, such as **karate** or **judo**. It's a sign of supreme accomplishment and suggests that the person is a master that you don't want to mess with. But the black belt for most marital arts is just another step on the journey. Many children have achieved the status of a black belt, and, in general, it can take about five years of practice and work to gain one; that is hardly "master" level. There are often degrees of black belts, or other colors that the practitioner can achieve. In Japanese, the black belt is called *shodan*, which means "first step," an acknowledgment that there is still much more to learn.

# Frankenstein is not the name of the monster.

Many people still get this confused, probably due to some old movie titles like *Frankenstein vs. Dracula and the Mummy*, or something similar. The classic film images give the impression of a tall figure stitched together with neck bolts who doesn't do much except growl and walk slowly. But in both movies and the original book, the name refers to the creature's creator, **Dr. Victor Frankenstein**. His creation has no name or is likened to **Adam**. Bonus misconception: the novel's monster is not created in a spooky castle, but rather in a nice apartment near the university where Victor is studying.

# The famed painting *American Gothic* depicts a father and daughter, not a married couple.

This well-known painting portrays a woman and a man standing in front of a farmhouse, dressed in conservative Middle American attire from the early twentieth century. Both people have stoic expressions and the man holds a pitchfork. It's often assumed that they are husband and wife, but the artist, **Grant Wood**, always intended for them to be father and daughter. They were modeled after the artist's sister, **Nan**, and his dentist, **Byron McKeeby**. McKeeby was in his sixties at the time, and Nan was in her thirties, so they were the correct ages to be a woman and her father.

# INDEX OF NAMES, TERMS, AND SHORT PHRASES

**Tim Rayborn** has written a large number of books and magazine articles about music, the arts, and history, as well as the strange and unusual; he will no doubt write more. He lived in England for many years and studied at the University of Leeds, which means he likes to pretend that he knows what he's talking about.

He's also an almost-famous musician who plays dozens of unusual instruments from all over the world that most people of have never heard of and usually can't pronounce.

He has appeared on more than forty recordings, and his musical wanderings and tours have taken him across the United States, all over Europe, to Canada and Australia, and to such romantic locations as Marrakech, Istanbul, Renaissance chateaux, medieval churches, and high school gymnasiums.

He currently lives in Northern California with many books, recordings, instruments, and a sometimes-demanding cat. He's pretty enthusiastic about cooking excellent food.

TimRayborn.com

# WHALEN
## BOOK · WORKS

Whalen Book Works is a small, independent book publishing company based in Kennebunkport, Maine, that combines top-notch design, unique formats, and fresh content to create truly innovative gift books.

Our unconventional approach to bookmaking is a close-knit, creative, and collaborative process among authors, artists, designers, editors, and booksellers. We publish a small, carefully curated list each season, and we take the time to make each book exactly what it needs to be.

We believe in giving back. That's why we plant one tree for every ten books we sell. Your purchase supports a tree in a United States national park.

*Get in touch!*

Visit us at **Whalenbooks.com**
or write to us at
68 North Street, Kennebunkport, ME 04046